100 POP / ROCK STARS

David Dachs

SCHOLASTIC BOOK SERVICES

New York Toronto London Auckland Sydney Tokyo

ISBN: 0-590-31366-5

Copyright © 1980 by David Dachs. All rights reserved. Published by Scholastic Book Services, a Division of Scholastic Magazines, Inc.

12 11 10 9 8 7 6 5 4 3 2 1   12   0 1 2 3 4 5/8

Printed in the U.S.A.   01

POP STARS: WHO CREATES THEM?

"A star ship's gold."
　　—Trade saying
Star: "An artistic performer or athlete whose leading role performance is acknowledged."
　　—American Heritage Dictionary of the English Language

Some of today's pop stars (the Bee Gees, Billy Joel, Paul McCartney, Donna Summer) are so big that if they put out a record on cardboard the record stations would play it. And the fans would buy it.

The way somebody or a group becomes a star is a form of box office democracy. The voting is clean, but it is mixed with high-powered media manipulation. You, the record buyer, vote at the record shop when you buy a disc or when you buy a ticket to a concert. Those who sell the most records and tapes and concert tickets are the stars.

Of course, shaping your taste and how you and your friends cast their votes are: 1) the disc jockeys, 2) the publicity people, 3) the song hits magazines, 4) the TV, 5) the best-seller lists. Where I live, the local record shop scotch-tapes best-seller lists from *Billboard*, *Cash Box*, and *Record World* on its windows. A none-too-subtle hint on what you should buy. So the voting is democratic, but there's a lot of media influences out there slanting your taste buds, and deciding who's up there on top.

The word "star," in the entertainment sense, probably goes back to World War I. That's when they began putting up gilded or silvered stars on the doors of dressing rooms of key actors and actresses. It took the pop hype machine to originate the word "superstar."

Today, the stars of pop music don't have stars on dressing rooms (usually they are on tour and stay no longer than a day in one place). But they have million-dollar contracts, high royalties, trust funds, accountants, and financial advisers. Many of them started out in their teens. They played guitars, sang a little in bars. They rehearsed in dirt-streaked little rehearsal studios. As they got into it, they realized that they were in a big business.

Very big business, indeed. In 1979 the modern record business, according to the Record Industry Association of America, grossed almost $4 billion. That's only for record sales. In the same year, Hollywood (all the motion pictures released) took in a record $2.6 billion in box office receipts. The record business is now bigger than the movies, in terms of dollar income.

This book is a collection of the key groups and personalities that dominate today's pop music. It's a collection of short biographies. It presents basic biographical data, some notes on the kind of music they perform or sing or create, along with mentions of their singles and albums. In other words, a handy reference book of personalities that have emerged as winners in the pop version of "star wars."

"Star wars" isn't an exaggerated term. Today's Grammy Award-winners, the gold record winners, have reached the top amid much fierce competition. And they find it hard to relax. They push themselves to go on still another tour, and another tour, even though they are tired and do not like "the road." The reason? Out there in some basement rec room, or in a rehearsal studio, there are other groups and personalities, practicing, planning, scheming to be the new Bee Gees, the new Linda Ronstadt.

Or as RSO Records put it in a full-page ad in *Billboard* (March 21, 1979):

> In this dog eat dog business
> RSO is out in front

Many of the stars included here "ship gold." That is, they presell $1 million worth of records and tapes to record dealers because of *anticipated demand*. These stars receive the highest royalty rates, the fattest concert and TV fees. Often the lyrics to their tunes are better known among young people than the works of Shakespeare, Robert Frost, or Langston Hughes.

In this book the stars and important musical bands are chosen because of: 1. *Popularity.* Sales of records, airplay, winning of awards, drawing power at concerts; 2. *Variety.* A desire to present all types of popular music (rock, soft rock, country, folk, soul, middle of the road pop, jazz, Latin-American; and 3. *Balance.* To present new and old names. Those still way up there after so many years are here, such as The Rolling Stones and Paul Simon, as well as the latest disco stars (Gloria Gaynor, The Village People).

Elvis Presley is omitted because he is no longer alive, but, of course, he continues to be a force in today's pop. Everybody in the book is active. Others have been dropped because they have little historical or musical interest. Sorry if your favorites are not written up. It would take a 2,000-page book to cover everybody.

A star/group has tremendous impact on speech, attitudes, clothes, home decorating. You walk around and see young people wearing T-shirts with the names of their favorite pop stars imprinted. Go into teenage bedrooms across America and you'll see color posters of The Rolling Stones, Donna Summer, John Travolta, Shaun Cassidy. Many kids wear Kiss key chains. TV producers use big pop names to win big ratings for drama shows.

Pop stars also have political clout. They are constantly wooed by candidates and political strategists to help raise money and build enthusiasm. Right before the terrible accident at the Three Mile

4

Island nuclear plant at Harrisburg, Pennsylvania, in March 1979, a spokesman for the nuclear industry said the campaign against nuclear power was inspired by some environmentalists and "pop singers."

And while I'm at it, I'd like to list some pet peeves.

1. *The constant rise in the cost of records.* Prices still may go higher with the Arabs raising oil prices. Oil is used in making the modern polyvinyl records. You should protest, but I don't know how. Got any ideas? 2. *Poor pressings.* A lot of the new releases by major companies are scratchy. If you buy one, don't be timid about returning defective recordings. 3. *Bad-mannered young people at concerts.* At a recent classic blues concert in famed Carnegie Hall in New York, fans brought in beer cans, scuffed the expensive carpets, and dangled their feet out of the boxes. No excuse for that. Nor for violence at rock shows.

The pop music industry needs to look into these things, and also to take some of its giant profits and put them into some worthwhile projects. In an interesting speech by Stan Cornyn, vice-president of Warner Brothers Records, he told NARM (National Association of Record Merchandisers): "We've hit it rich. We've sold more records and takes than Burma has sold of anything . . . . We have captured and even dominated the imagination of our customers like no other group, with the possible exception of the Catholic clergy in the Middle Ages. We must do more for culture for generations yet to come than the Country Music Wax Museum."

He added, "Our success need not be measured only by how many [records] we sell. We have the clear opportunity to do something about the quality of life around us."

In plain words, it means that they could do more. As Cornyn said, "Take a little, leave a little."

One final take. Young people have picked pop music as their form of culture, their entertainment. The college generation seems to have fastened onto films, with a secondary interest in pop. While studies have shown that people in their thirties, middle-aged, and older people buy lots of pop music in all forms (records, sheet music, tickets to pop concerts, film musicals, Broadway musicals, straw hat musicals), teen-agers are the most faithful buyers of day-to-day pop releases. It's teen-agers' money that sustains the giant record companies — RCA, Columbia, MCA, Warners, A & M, RSO, Motown.

Young people identify with the pop stars and pop music. The pop sounds cushion them from the harsh world outside; sometimes the harsh sounds represent certain anger. The words provide facts about emotions and feelings that interest them. Somehow young people feel that the pop stars speak their language about love, sex, growing up, parents, and the Establishment (whoever that is).

Of course, young people buy a lot of musical junk food—hack melodies covered over by rock arrangements and studio gimmicks. Much of what is said in lyrics is trite and on the level of TV soap opera. Punk rock lyrics are far more realistic, sharper, anarchistic. But there's hardly any love or kindness there; and where are the good tunes?

Good or bad, it's a new world. Huck Finn used to amuse himself with boyhood adventures, floating downriver on a raft. Today's youngsters amuse themselves with a hi-fi set and float on waves of sound.

ABBA

★

Some call them the Beatles of Sweden. The quartet (two boys, two girls) met while they were doing back-up vocals in a record studio. They are: Annifrid Lyngstad, Benny Andersson, Bjorn Ulvaeus, and Agnetha Falksong Ulvaeus. Bjorn and Agnetha are married, and have a daughter. Agnetha started singing with a dance orchestra in 1965. At 11, Bjorn played banjo and guitar in a dance band. Benny toured with a Swedish group of the sixties, the Hep Stars. At 10, Annifrid made her first appearance as a singer on a Swedish TV program.

In 1975 this pop group got its first taste of success when a song composed by two of its members (Benny and Bjorn), "Waterloo," won a top award in the Eurovision Song Festival. Their early recordings were on a label called Polar Music. They have had a streak of global hits in Europe and Australia. Altantic Records, which distributes ABBA in the USA, has claimed that ABBA, during 1974–78, sold more than 50 million records

around the world. Last Christmas, they were chosen to appear on the giant TV UNICEF concert organized by the Bee Gees, *A Gift of Life,* over NBC to help poor children.

Their first American LP was *Waterloo* and the first singles put out here were "Honey Honey" and "Ring Ring." The two girls are cute to look at, and wholesome. ABBA is one of Sweden's most profitable enterprises, along with modern furniture and glassware. They've done some U.S. TV, but not much. Not only has ABBA sold well at the record counters, but they have won the respect of picky hard-core rock fanatics. Their skill in the studio is such that some say they rank with such record producers as Brian Wilson of the Beach Boys and Phil Spector.

Among their smash singles are "SOS," "I Do, I Do, I Do, I Do," "Mama Mia," "Fernando," and "Dancing Queen." The first U.S. gold record was *ABBA's Greatest Hits.*

In 1978, ABBA came out with a rock film called *ABBA — The Movie.* It has been released around the world. There are close-ups of the group performing, along with audience hysteria (á la the Beatles' *A Hard Day's Night*). It also has a slight story line and fantasy sequences.

Back-to-back the group also issued an LP titled *ABBA — The Album,* which was close to "a concept album" (an LP that develops one theme). The nine songs ranged from driving rockers to lyrical ballads. Among the cuts: "Eagle," "The Girl with the Golden Hair," and "The Name of the Game." The last leaped onto the U.S. charts.

AEROSMITH

★

You heard them in the film *Sgt. Pepper's Lonely Hearts Club Band* and on Columbia Records. It's a group that came out of nowhere with little advance hype. Aerosmith started out in 1970 playing for $30 a night. They played in clubs, such as The Barn in New Hampshire, and little resorts. They also played a lot of one-nighters in New England. At one time, they even played on the streets of Boston, for free. These gigs and appearances helped build up their name and helped them create a strong New England following. By '72 they were almost as popular as clam chowder and the Boston Red Sox.

Musically, it's a five-man hard-rock outfit. Reviewing one of its LPs, *Billboard* wrote that "it works best live." The group does contemporary rock, R & B, and medleys of vintage hits such as "I Ain't You" and "Mother Popcorn." Most of the original material performed by the group is by Steven Tyler (lyrics) and Joe Perry (music). *Variety*, too, looks at them as performers of "high decibel rock." A review of a two-LP set, *Aerosmith Live — Bootleg* (Nov. 1978), describes them as "one of the most popular of the U.S. rock groups, famed for its ear-shattering disks."

Onstage live, Aerosmith is a bundle of electronic dynamite. In August of 1978, *Blast,* a music newsletter, reported that the Eastern band really rocked fans in two big concert appearances out West. "Aerosmith has blown 'em out of two big ones this past summer — first it was Cal-Jam, and then at the beginning of July at the Texxas [yes, two x's] World Music Festival." The powerhouse vocalist of the group is Steven Tyler. Some compare him to jumping Mick Jagger.

Aerosmith released its first LP in 1973 under the simple title, *Aerosmith.* Its founding members: Steven Tyler (vocals), Joe Perry (lead guitarist), Brad Whitford (rhythm and lead guitar), Tom Hamilton (bass), and Joey Kramer (drums). Its gold records include: *Get Your Wings, Toys in the Attic,* and *Rocks.*

Late in '78, Aerosmith members complained to *Circus* Magazine that radio is putting down their brand of heavy rock in favor of a softer "marshmallow rock." They feel that music programmers of radio stations are discriminating against the loud sound. Meanwhile, however, they haven't suffered any depression. They continue to cut records and do personal appearances.

PAUL ANKA

An eager-beaver and over-achiever, at 13 Paul Anka was in Los Angeles recording his first song. That was quite a thing, since Paul's home was in Canada. The single on RPM Records "stiffed out," he says. He returned to Ottawa a failure. At 16 he went knocking on the doors of ABC Records in New York City with four of his songs. One was called "Diana." It was reportedly about his brother's baby-sitter.

Released as a single, "Diana" went straight to the top. He continued with other teen-type hits: "You Are My Destiny," "Puppy Love," and "Lonely Boy," all sung in an over-sentimental, purplish manner. At 19, the 5'4" compact singer-songwriter became a pop millionaire.

Then the music business changed. Hard rock and the Beatles came along. Paul's career stalled. He wondered if he would ever have hits again. He also worried over the fact that adults would only see him as a mild rock and roll singer of sticky teen-age pop. "I was living on my past," he says.

In 1968 somebody showed Paul a French ballad, *"Comme d'habitude* (In The Usual Way)." He bought the rights and wrote a new English lyric. Frank Sinatra recorded it because it fit him like a glove. The song, "My Way," was a grown-up song about individuality and finding your own way in life. It was a smash. Adult audiences looked at Anka differently. He could play the big clubs, TV. He was back in the limelight.

All in all, this Canadian songwriter has written more than 400 songs. He wrote "She's A Lady" for Tom Jones, and material cut by Andy Williams, Sonny and Cher, and The Fifth Dimension. He has also created TV themes (one used by the *Tonight Show*) and the title song of the film *The Longest Day*. Recently, his own career as an RCA recording artist has been revitalized. He's had a streak of hits, including, "You're Having My Baby," and "The Times Of Your Life." Today he is more successful than ever. He does night clubs, appears on TV, and does concerts around the world.

Anka was born on July 30, 1941, in Ottawa, Canada. His parents, both Lebanese-Canadians, operated restaurants. He is still a Candian citizen. In 1978 he was awarded an honorary doctor of music degree by St. John's University in Queens, New York.

The singer-songwriter-businessman-music publisher loves to wear big cowboy hats. He is married to a former model. They have five children. Paul is a devoted father.

He has two homes, one in Carmel, California, and the other in Las Vegas. He has a private jet and he is a partner in a new million-dollar discotheque, Jubilation, in Las Vegas. He considers the most important part of his talent to be his songwriting. That skill now accounts for a third of his income. His RCA bio states, "It's been over two decades since Paul Anka emerged as a rock and roll teen-age prodigy. Now he's very much an adult phenomenon." That's no exaggeration.

On LP: *His Best* (U.A.), *Listen To Your Heart* (RCA), *Vintage Years* (SIRE), *Remember Diana, Songs I Wish I'd Written, Paul Anka—21 Golden Hits, This Is Love.*

ASHFORD &
SIMPSON

Boy meets girl. Boy gets girl. It still happens, and it happened with Nick Simpson. At the age of 21, he saw 17-year-old Valerie on stage in Harlem. "I was standing there when I looked and saw Valerie. She put me in a spin, she was such a beautiful girl. There was something about the way she moved and sang. I had to know her." Today Nick Ashford and Valerie Simpson are married and have a child.

Besides being husband and wife, they are recording stars for Warner Bros. Records. Once they worked behind the scenes as writers and producers. Now they write and produce and perform. Musically, they come out of the pop soul tradition. The lyrics they write are simple and generally deal with love. In the beginning they had a way of adding little arranging figures and "riffs" to tunes. Later on they started to write their own songs.

Feeling that there was good money to be made in pop, they made a connection with Glover Records and later with Scepter Records. With Scepter, a small label that introduced Dionne Warwick, they knocked out their first hit, the national anthem of the drug culture, "Let's Get Stoned," which was recorded by Ray Charles. A Motown official heard the tune, found out who wrote and produced it, and invited them to come to Detroit as writer-producers.

In those hectic days, they wrote, arranged, and helped edit the tapes for Marvin Gaye, Tammi Terrell, and Diana Ross. Among the chart-toppers they were associated with were "Ain't No Mountain High Enough" and "Reach Out and Touch (Somebody's Hand)."

In the late sixties Valerie branched out as a vocalist on albums with Quincy Jones. She recorded two solo albums, *Exposed* and *Valerie Simpson*. A single from the second LP turned into an R & B hit, "Silly, Wasn't It?" Valerie then decided to record with her songwriting partner, Nick. By this time, the two had departed from Motown.

In 1977 they cut their fifth Warner Bros. LP, *Send It*, which they also wrote and arranged. From it came three chart hits: "Don't Cost You Nothin'," "By Way of Love's Express," and "Send It." It became the duo's first gold album. (Their first LP for Warner Bros. was *Gimme Something Real* in 1973.)

In 1978 they played the Palace on Broadway and got a royal welcome. The *New York Post* wrote: "The Palace is where they belong. The show is slick and slinky, their music, the rhythm and blues kind that, whether ballad or rocker, has a musical thrust. The audience particularly ate up 'Gimme Something Real.' "

Valerie plays the piano and is dazzling to look àt. Ashford has a mustache, a beard, and a sweet smile. Together they are a potent pop team. They made history with Motown as producers, arrangers, and songwriters. Now they continue to cut top-ten records on their own. On LP: *Is It, Send It,* and *So Satisfied* (all on Warner Bros.).

JOAN BAEZ

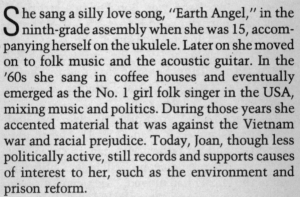

S he sang a silly love song, "Earth Angel," in the ninth-grade assembly when she was 15, accompanying herself on the ukulele. Later on she moved on to folk music and the acoustic guitar. In the '60s she sang in coffee houses and eventually emerged as the No. 1 girl folk singer in the USA, mixing music and politics. During those years she accented material that was against the Vietnam war and racial prejudice. Today, Joan, though less politically active, still records and supports causes of interest to her, such as the environment and prison reform.

In 1978, for example, there was a TV special, *Sing-Sing-Thanksgiving.* On the show were several stars presenting a concert for prisoners, among them, Joan Baez. Some say she's changed a bit, that she's less intense. However, her voice is still cool, clear, and compelling. Of singing Miss Baez once said, "To sing is to love, to affirm, to fly and soar."

Most of her earlier works — hit albums and singles — were on Vanguard. These include *Any Day Now, Best of Joan Baez, David's First Album, First Ten Years, Folk Songs,* and *In Concert.* Not long ago, she moved on to A & M Records. Some critics think she's become more commerical, more hit-minded in recent years. In fact, she's been a headliner in Las Vegas, the glittering home of slot machines and gambling. Her more recent albums for A & M: *Best of Joan Baez, Blowin' Away, From Every State, Lovesong Album.* Perhaps her biggest single was "The Night They Drove Old Dixie Down."

At one time, she was Bob Dylan's girlfriend. Later she married David Harris, an anti-war activist. Divorced from Mr. Harris, she is now the mother of a child. In 1978, she appeared in a Bob Dylan feature film, *Renaldo and Clara.* She's a fan of Dylan's songs. "To me, Dylan shines above everybody else," she says.

The black-haired, attractive Ms. Baez was born on Staten Island, N.Y., Jan. 9, 1941. Her mother is English, and her father, Mexican, is a physicist. She first met prejudice in Redlands, California, where the family had moved. "Mexican kids were looked down on. And Mexican kids didn't like me because I didn't speak Spanish."

She was at Woodstock, the great, muddy rock love and peace festival of '69. Before hundreds of thousands, she stood on stage and sang many songs including the classic "Joe Hill." The song told of the death of an IWW (International Workers of the World) organizer who was trying to help workers

20

win better conditions. The lyrics she sang stressed that the only way to fight injustice is to band together. The line goes: "Don't mourn for me — organize." Joan also has written a very good autobiography, *Daybreak*.

THE BEACH BOYS

Back in the pre-rock days, there was a singing group, The Four Freshmen, that recorded on Capitol. It sang Tin Pan Alley songs with fresh, inventive, four-part harmony. It shaped the Beach Boys sound. Al Jardine once told *Circus*, "I bumped into Brian [Wilson] on campus one day. Smash-o. So we went into the music room between classes and sang Four Freshmen songs." One of the songs they did, a favorite of Brian's, was "Polka Dot and Moonbeams."

When the Beach Boys started in 1961, they were known as the Pendletones. The themes they chose for lyrics were the teen California scene, the beaches, the summer sun, and young love. In 1962, the first record they made was about the new craze, "Surfin'." Produced by a small label, Candix, the record sold pretty well in California. But Candix folded. Then Murray Wilson, the father of the Wilson boys (Carl, Denis, and Brian), got them a contract on Capitol.

On that label they emerged as one of the top

22

groups in the U.S. Its key members, along with the Wilson brothers, were Al Jardine and Mike Love. In a biography, *The Beach Boys*, John Tobler said that they "created their own individual and highly distinctive sound based on close harmonies, rolling melodies, and brilliantly evocative lyrics." To others, it wasn't so much that the teen-slanted lyrics were so great, but they gave off positive vibrations. What one critic called "fun-fun-fun music."

In the '60s the radio throbbed with Beach Boys songs. These songs celebrated the outdoor, sun-filled, problem-free world of mythical high school students. Their lyrics were full of lines like "She's head cheerleader, she dates the quarterback," and "Be true to your school, just as you would to your girl and guy." No protest songs, just the endless summer of adolescence, where your problems were solved by a ride over the waves.

In the creative sense, Brian has been the leader, though other members have created songs too. He wrote, he arranged, he provided the high, clear falsetto. Later on, Brian turned to more serious and moodier themes, that of solitude, as in the song "In My Room." But they still stuck close, in those early days, to young people's interests. One LP, *Little Deuce Coupe*, focused on cars.

As the years went by, the Beach Boys added Bruce Johnson, Daryl Dragon, and others. People came and went. Types of songs changed. They spent a lot of time in the studio. One song, "Good Vibrations," took 6 months to produce. In addition, there were many personal crises and several of the Beach Boys took to the new psychologies around to clear their heads and fight stress. They began mediating. Mike Love and Al Jardine went to Spain to become teachers of TM (Transcendental Meditation). Carl and Denis took est. Brian got onto drugs and for a while was out of it.

Today the Beach Boys continue to be active. In 1977 they cut an LP covering fifteen years of music-making, *Fifteen Big Ones*. In 1979 they toured and even got on the disco kick, recording one number, "Here Comes the Night," that lasted nearly 11 minutes for a new LP, *L.A.*

On LP: *Pet Sounds* (with "wall to wall" sounds), *Surf's Up*, *Good Vibrations*. Their hit singles include: "I Can Hear Music," "Surfin', USA," "Fun, Fun, Fun," "Had to Phone Ya."

GEORGE BENSON

Jazz seldom makes it to the Top 10, which is dominated by rock. Pop stations ignore the discs of fine jazz singers and instrumentalists (cool, hot, and subtle). Disc jockeys play them at home, but don't play them on the air. These records are mostly heard on small-signal jazz stations and public radio. In this way, the mainstream USA is cut off from musicians working in this native American artform. One exception is brown-eyed George Benson, of Tenafly, New Jersey. A Warner Bros. artist, he's cracked through radio's vinyl curtain to the top of the pop charts with his jazz/pop style.

A guitarist with a swinging, mellow singing voice, George had a number-one single, "This Masquerade." In 1976 he really broke through with *Breezin'*, on Warner Bros. Records. It turned out to be the biggest selling jazz album of all time so far, a Double Platinum record (more than 2 million sold). That LP brought him three Grammys as Best Jazz Artist and Best Jazz Album in

'76 and '77. His own success may pave the way for other jazz singers/musicians.

A native of Pittsburgh, George began playing the guitar at the age of 8. He actually played record dates for RCA at 10. As a young man, he worked as a vocalist with a number of Pittsburgh R & B groups. As years went by, he cut records for Columbia and A & M Records.

In the mid-sixties, Benson was typed as a jazz guitarist. Those years he recorded for Creed Taylor and CTI, an independent label. "While I was at CTI, they didn't want me to sing, they just wanted me to play the guitar. A lot of people never knew I could sing because I just wasn't given the opportunity to express myself vocally," he says.

As a CTI recording artist, Benson's eloquent and subtle guitar style brought him moderate success. He did a number of solos in a Grammy-nominated album, *White Rabbitt.* He added to his reputation with a succession of guest album appearances with such jazz luminaries as Freddie Hubbard, Ron Carter, Hubert Laws, Herbie Hancock, Esther Philips, and Miles Davis.

The success of *Breezin'* has made him a brand name in pop. On the strength of that LP, he has appeared on TV *(Saturday Night Live)* and in concert. His records now sell all over the world, including Europe, Japan, and Australia.

In 1978 Benson took on Broadway. He put on his own show at the Belasco Theatre called simply "On Broadway." Ticket demand was so heavy he was forced to do a two-week run. One reviewer wrote that Benson "spins out some of the classier mood music around." Nowadays, he plays an electric guitar as well as an acoustic one. The *New York Post* called him a cool "laid-back Benson." It also praised him for putting on a show that accented music, not fancy, costly production effects. It went on: "Benson played his predictable run of top 40 stuff ("The Greatest Love of All," "This Masquerade"), but also did manage to sneak in some nice jazz runs and vocal scat between the cracks.

His LPs include: *In Flight* and *Weekend in L.A.*, his first live album, a double record set. (Incidentally, a live album is something recorded before an audience, not in a recording studio.)

THE BEE GEES

"We want to make people happy," says Maurice Gibb. He and his brothers Barry and Robin seem to have that knack. In 1979 they continue to be smoking hot. After the most successful album of all time, *Saturday Night Fever* (25 million so far), they issued *Spirits Having Flown*. Without a movie behind it, the LP raced right up to the top. And not only that, a single from the album, "Tragedy," raced up to number one on the charts too. That adds up to some kind of record, say pop statisticians. The Bee Gees are the first group in the last 10 years to have five consecutive singles reach number one on the sales charts. So far, the Bee Gees have had eight number-one singles during their career, more than any other recording artist/group in the '70s.

The Bee Gees reportedly do not read music. That's an advantage and a disadvantage. The advantage is that they come up with the sort of melodies perhaps they couldn't dream up if they were formally trained. Anyhow, they have emerged

29

as the successors to the Beatles. They are: 1) record stars, 2) songwriters, and 3) they also create material and act as producers for other recording artists. Maurice has produced an Osmond Brothers album, and Barry has produced LPs for his younger brother, Andy.

The Bee Gees record for RSO. They put down their instrumental and vocal tracks in Miami's Criteria Studios. Barry and Maurice live in Florida. Robin comes to Florida for the record sessions but makes his home in a house outside of London. He also has a home in Connecticut. Barry and Lynda Gibb have two children, Stephen, 6, and Ashley, 1½. Robin and Molly Gibb (she once worked for RSO Records chief, Robert Stigwood, as a secretary) have two children also, Spencer, 6, and Melissa, 5.

Musically, the Bee Gees believe in commerical mainstream pop music. They do ballads, some R & B, soft-rock, disco, and even songs with lush settings. Their themes are mostly about love. They rarely probe new thoughts. In their vocal approach, they mostly stress falsetto lead vocals sung by Barry. In the rock spectrum, they are MOR — middle of the road.

The oldest is Barry, born Douglas, Isle of Man, England, Sept. 1, 1947. Maurice and Robin are twins, born in Manchester, England, Dec. 22, 1949. Their father, Hugh, worked as a pop dance band musician. One day he heard his sons sing. He liked what he heard and got them jobs. They'd get up in short pants and long white socks and sing British favorites, music hall tunes, and some American pop hits. According to an English reporter, "By the time Barry was eight and the twins were five, they were right in there with Dad belting out Irving Berlin's 'Alexander's Ragtime Band.' "

In 1958 the Gibb family moved to Australia, where the Gibb boys sang on the radio on a show called *Anything Goes.* Later they had their own TV show. They also performed on *Australian Bandstand,* where they sang and imitated American rock stars. In 1962 they signed with Festival Records; their first single was "Three Kisses of Love." In 1967 they took a boat to London, where they met and signed with Robert Stigwood, an Australian record and music executive who has skillfully guided the Bee Gees through the years and gave them the assignment to write (and perform) the songs for the film *Saturday Night Fever.*

Bee Gee singles: "How Deep Is Your Love," "Stayin' Alive," "Edge of the Universe," "Boogie Child," "Words," "New York Mining Disaster, 1941," "I Can't See Nobody," and "Tragedy." On LP: *Bee Gees Live, Saturday Night Fever* (soundtrack), *Spirits Having Flown.*

BLONDIE

Their fame comes not only from their music, but from their outrageous stage routines and the feeling they give an audience that they might do anything. The unexpected is expected.

Blondie consists of guitarist Frank Infante; drummer Clem Burke; keyboardist Jimmy Destri; bassist Nigel Harrison; guitarist Chris Stein; and lead singer, co-founder, and co-composer, Debbie Harry.

There is no question that this 34-year-old, 5'3" ex-Bunny wins most of Blondie's publicity. She was born in Miami and adopted by a Hawthorne, N.J., couple (Richard and Catherine Harry) when she was three months old. Debbie and her younger sister, Martha, were given piano and dance lessons. As a teenager Debbie hung around Manhattan's East Village during the flower-power era and eventually sang with a folk group called Wind In The Willows. She also supplemented her income by painting, writing, and taking odd jobs as secretary, barmaid, beautician, and Playboy Bunny. In 1968 the group folded and she went into a depression that led to drugs.

But in 1973 Debbie pulled herself together and joined a three-woman group, the Stilettoes. Around this same time a friend introduced her to Chris Stein, a Brooklynite, and it was love at first sight. Together they spent a year forming various bands, and finally came up with the band which they named after the color of her hair. Now, seven years later they still live together in a three-room penthouse (with a tiger-striped kitchen floor) on the West Side of Manhattan. "We never rip each other off," says Stein.

In the beginning Blondie was known as a punk rock band due to the raw-sounding music and Debbie's thrift-shop costumes and wild hairdo. Recently she's done the glamour bit and they've been even more successful. Musically, they've incorporated disco. They are expanding their activities.

Blondie is the first group to perform a whole LP for videotape cassettes. It's called *Eat to the Beat*, and Debbie has starred in a film, *Union City*, as a New Jersey housewife.

Both Debbie and the rest of Blondie, together with Meat Loaf, are in a movie titled *Roadie*. It was released in the summer of 1980, and is the story of a truck driver, played by Meat Loaf, who falls for a groupie and becomes a "roadie." Blondie is the band for which he roadies.

With her skintight jumpsuits and spike heels, Debbie is rock's number one pinup. *The New York Times'* critic, John Rockwell, describes her as having "awkwardly endearing klutzishness."

They are the first progressive new-wave rockers to make it in the mainstream market and last summer had an SRO 27-city cross-country tour. Most of them come to see Debbie — a woman who's been there and makes no bones about it — with the lyric, "When I met you in the restaurant/ You could tell I was no debutante."

In the record industry's worst slump in 25 years their disco-like single, "Heart of Glass," went platinum and the LP, *Parallel Lines*, has sold more than five million worldwide. Another monster single seller for the group was "One Way Or Another."

Complete list of Blondie albums to date: *Parallel Lines, Blondie, Plastic Letters,* and *Eat to the Beat.*

DEBBY BOONE

D aughter of singer Pat Boone and granddaughter of country and western star Red Foley, Debby has known about show business since she could skip and hop. She was born in Hackensack, New Jersey, in 1957. When she was 4 her family moved to Los Angeles. She is one of four girls. Her mother, Shirley Boone, dressed her four daughters alike (there's Cherry, Lindy, and Laury, as well as Debby), and taught them to sing four-part harmony. As a youngster she sang at church socials and also with her father on tour in a sort of singing Boone family show.

As a teenager, Debby was the most rebellious of the four Boone girls. She came out of her "adolescing" closer to her parents than ever, particularly to her father. After graduating Marymount High School, she worked with emotionally disturbed children for a year as a volunteer. Then she attended Bible school for a year and a half. At the same time, she never completely forgot her singing. One day she told her parents that she wanted to have a career in show business. She says, "My father told me it was a hard life for a girl, but he never did say, 'Please don't do it.' "

Debby had to go it alone. Her sisters (two married, and one in college) were unable to go on tours as they once had. Enter Mike Curb, record producer. For three years he had been after her to turn solo. When she said "okay" he cut her first Warner/Curb single. It was just a little song called "You Light Up My Life," the theme song from a low-budget Columbia film of the same name. An album with the same title was also released in which Debby's sisters sang backup.

The heavens opened up, commercially speaking. The single zoomed to number one. At the 1978 Grammy Awards, Debby and "You Light Up My Life" won Best New Artist and Song of the Year. "You Light Up My Life" was an Academy Award-winner as well for Best Song of the Year. She also received a retailers award (NARM) for Best Selling Single and Best Selling LP by a New Artist. It is odd that in the so-called dominance of rock the public went for a simple Tin Pan Alley-ish ballad like Debby's "You Light Up My Life."

An easygoing girl with a sense of humor, Debby has a good strong voice. She's good to look at, an attractive, wholesome, All-American girl type. She's not one of the "wild ones." On stage she's relaxed. A devout Christian, she often performs for church-related functions without pay. Her favorite singers include Barbra Streisand, Linda Ronstadt, and Emmylou Harris.

In her second album, *Midstream*, she did a lot of soft, contemporary pop by such songwriters as

Neil Sedaka. A frequent guest on TV, she has appeared on a variety of programs, including *The Tonight Show, Dinah!, American Bandstand, A Tribute to Elizabeth Taylor,* and *A Salute to Israel's 30th Birthday.* You can reach Debby at Warner/Curb Records, 3300 Warner Blvd., Burbank, CA 91505.

DAVID BOWIE

David Bowie has a son named "Zowie." It may be a nickname, but it's a wild one. And if so, it's natural because David Bowie is a controversial, theatrical RCA star. He wears odd clothes, uses blasting stage light and odd makeup. One season he may have whitish hair. The next season he may appear on stage in flaming orange hair. His taste in clothes runs from Zoot suits with baggy pants and lizard jackets to shiny space-age suits.

Such hairstyles and "plastic" clothes are meant to be dramatic. They depict characters and ideas that Bowie wants his audience to think about. Bowie, mostly, is down on modern society.

His real name is David Robert Jones. He was born in Brixton, South London, England, in 1947. He quit school at 16, and worked as a commercial artist. Later he formed a pop group called David Jones and the Lower Third. In 1963 he cut his first record. When an album of his didn't do too well he decided to become a Buddhist monk and went to a retreat in Scotland. He retreated from the retreat to return to pop and its jangly existence. In 1969 he had his first hit single, "Space Oddity."

As a pop star he was expected to function on the hype circuit, visit deejays, etc. He didn't like that. So he opened up an arts lab. But that didn't last long either. This Bowie is a restless guy. During this period he also got involved in the art of mime. At the end of '69 he returned to the recording studio and cut an album that turned into a whopping hit, *The Man Who Sold the World*. It portrayed a cold world. Bowie punched out the songs in what RCA calls "enormous defiant energy."

The theatrical side of Bowie emerged strongly in another LP, *The Rise and Fall of Ziggy Stardust and The Spiders from Mars*, the story of a fallen rock star. In concert, David Bowie became the flamboyant, wild rock star. He wore white makeup, stacked boots, dyed hair that came from the stylized Kabuki Theatre of Japan. "Off stage I'm a robot," he said. "On stage I achieve emotion. It's probably why I prefer Ziggy to David."

Later on he dipped into George Orwell's novel, *1984*, and came up with a brutal picture of society in his LP, *Diamond Dogs*. It is clear from these and other works, that he is a rock actor-producer, mixing music with sociology and theater. He also has experimented with chance-writing, going with thoughts even though they do not follow in sequence.

Along with recording his rock visions, he has appeared in a film, *The Man Who Fell to Earth*. Other Bowie LPs include: *Heroes, Station to Station, Low*.

JACKSON
BROWNE

Singer-songwriter-guitarist-record producer. He was born in Heidelberg, Germany, on Oct. 9, 1948. When he was 3 his family moved to Los Angeles. As a young boy he was attracted to music, and learned how to play the piano and guitar. During high school, he wrote songs, played in coffeehouses, and joined up, briefly, with the Nitty Gritty Dirt Band.

In 1967 Jackson went to New York with two friends in an old station wagon. There he got a job as an accompanist to Nico, who had just left the Velvet Underground. Next year he made another trip to New York without setting the pop world on fire. At the same time he started to market his songs to Linda Ronstadt, Johnny Rivers, and the Byrds. In 1970 he went on his first concert tour, opening the show for Laura Nyro.

In 1972 a new independent label with a weird

name, Asylum Records, gave him a chance to do a solo album, *Jackson Browne*. The LP hit the charts, and right after that he went on a tour with Joni Mitchell. In the fall of '72, Jackson went on his own concert tour, assisted by David Lindley, a West Coast studio musician. *For Everyman*, Browne's second LP, did well and then *Late for the Sky*, his third album, went gold.

Jackson Browne's career was doing fine the next few years, and he got married. In 1977 his wife committed suicide. That smashed him up. He took time off to think, rest, but found the best medicine was to work, work, work.

Slender, good-looking, and in his early 30s, Browne has gone through a lot. Recent publicity shots show him wearing mod glasses and a sad-eyed expression. Browne works in a folk/rock/country vein. He's written many songs about the natives of California, personal relationships, the world of the rock tours ("The Load-Out"), and the rock performer. One goes:

> Everyone I know, everywhere I go
> People need some reason to believe
> I don't know about anyone, but me
> If it takes this night, that'll be all right
> If I can get you to smile before I leave

Jackson is also co-author of a pro and con song about drugs, "Cocaine." Since 1976 he has acted as record producer for Warren Zevon *(Warren Zevon)*. The pop star performs at benefit concerts for causes he believes in, notably environment groups such as the Sierra Club and the Dolphin Project.

In December 1977, Elektra/Asylum released his

fifth album, *Running On Empty*. So far, it's his biggest selling LP—a platinum record. He is co-author of many of the songs. The ten-tune LP was recorded during a summer tour in Holiday Inn hotel rooms, on buses, backstage and onstage. The *Hit Parader* called it "Jackson's most powerful, articulate, and entertaining LP to date."

His best known songs: "Doctor My Eyes," "Rock Me on the Water," "These Days," "Song For Adam," "For Everyman," "Fountain of Sorrow," "Before the Deluge," "Here Come Those Tears," "Late for the Sky" (inserted in film, *Taxi Driver*), "Take It Easy (The Eagles first hit; co-author). Browne on LP: *Jackson Browne, Late for the Sky, Running on Empty*.

GLEN CAMPBELL

In 1979, at the 21st Annual Grammy Awards, Glen Campbell was a "presenter." He "sang" his dialogue and gave away Grammys. That's the role they give to people who have made a solid contribution to the world of recordings. And he has. Some of the classics of modern country music were made popular by this six-foot, good-looking, blue-eyed singer-guitarist. They include such favorites as: "By the Time I Get to Phoenix," "Gentle on My Mind," "Wichita Lineman."

He continues to have current hits too. Not long ago, he had a monster smash, "Rhinestone Cowboy." When he's not making records or appearing on TV, Glen pursues the active life. He keeps in shape with his favorite sports — golf, hunting, fishing, and water-skiing. He even sponsors a golf tournament, the Glen Campbell Open.

His roots are country music, but mixed in it are modern arrangements, and songs that are warm without being drippy tearjerkers. He's got a likeable personality and a homespun baritone. There's a touch of Las Vegas in him, but he still hangs onto his downhome basics. He's been a hit maker since the 1960s on Capitol Records.

He was born April 10, 1938, in a town with a beautiful name: Delight, Arkansas. Glen got into music when his father gave him a mail-order guitar. By the time he was 6 he had become a musical prodigy, singing and stroking his guitar on radio shows throughout a three-state area. At the same time, he worked hard as one of 12 kids in a big farm family. "I picked cotton for $1.25 a hundred pounds," he once recalled. "If you worked your tail off you could pick 80 or 90 pounds a day. Except my pa. He could pick 400 pounds a day."

Music, though, played a big part in his childhood. "Everybody in my family played and sang. We sang in church, songs like " 'Where Could I Go But to the Lord,' " he says.

As a teenager, young Campbell joined his first band, a Western group headed by his uncle, and later formed his own band. At the insistence of friends he went to Hollywood where, after a few weeks, he made his first recording for an independent record company. This first date led to many more, and Campbell soon established himself as a top studio musician. By 1961 his singing ability had become almost as well-known as his instrumental talent and he made several records which attained the best-seller list. In 1967 his recording of "Gentle on My Mind" was an overnight smash, followed immediately by another big hit, "By the Time I Get to Phoenix." Both won

Grammy Awards for the young singer-instrumentalist. He co-starred in the film, *True Grit*.

His LPs include: *By the Time I Get to Phoenix, Gentle on My Mind, Basic, Live at the Royal Festival Hall, Southern.*

THE CAPTAIN
AND TENNILLE

Both of them come from show biz families. Toni's father was a singer with a 1940s swing band, Bob Crosby's Bobcats. And Daryl's father, Carmen Dragon, was (and is) a conductor and arranger, known for his concerts at the Hollywood Bowl. Together they make up The Captain and Tennille. She does the warm, strong vocals; writes songs. He does the clever arrangements and plays a variety of instruments, including keyboard. They are married and they record for A & M Records. In '76 they had their own TV show on ABC. In March 1979, they produced an ambitious, highly praised TV special on ABC mixing the blues, Broadway, Bach, and rock.

How they broke through is a classic case history of do-it-yourself. The two were playing small clubs in California in 1973. In September of that year, they went into a small studio in the San Fernando

Valley, no bigger than those fast photo booths in dime stores, and cut a record. A love song, called "The Way I Want to Touch You." They spent $250 to press 500 copies. They sent them to local radio stations. On the record, Daryl played all the instruments, and Toni did all the vocal parts. Without a major record label backing and no formal distributor, the record rocketed to become a hit. A & M Records then stepped into the picture, purchased the record, and signed them.

Toni Tennille was born on May 8, 1943, in Montgomery, Alabama. She was very active in school clubs at Sidney Lanier H.S. She studied classical piano as a child for nine years. Two of her sisters, Louisa and Melissa, occasionally tour with her and Daryl, and sing background vocals. The family moved to Los Angeles in 1962; they've been in L.A. ever since. Toni's first job was as a file clerk.

Her entry into popular music came when she joined the South Coast Repertory Theatre. She and the group's director then went ahead and wrote a rock ecology musical, *Mother Earth*. The show ran successfully in San Francisco to good reviews and even had a short engagement in Los Angeles before going on to New York, where it failed. For the L.A. run the show needed a new keyboard player. Enter Daryl Dragon, who was in town in-between Beach Boy tours.

Daryl Dragon, a talented musician, has been associated with music all his life. Born Aug. 27, 1942, he grew up in Los Angeles with two brothers and two younger sisters. He studied classical piano for 10 years. He first performed with his brothers,

Dennis and Doug. The three young Dragons actually recorded an album for Capitol where their father, Carmen Dragon, has recorded all his symphony albums and light "pops" LPs. The album was not very successful. Daryl says, "The Beatles came in just as we released the album and we lost hope. We were an instrumental group and you had to sing to get any jobs."

He then met Toni during the Los Angeles run of *Mother Earth* and was impressed with her writing and singing. A strong friendship grew into marriage. Once an overweight teenager, Toni is now lean. She and Daryl are vegetarians. They eat only eggs and dairy foods; no meat of any kind. On tour they carry most of their food supplies with them — granola, nuts, raisins, brown rice. They live in Pacific Palisades, California.

Their hit singles include: "I Just Want to Touch You" (composed by Toni), "Love Will Keep Us Together." On LP: *Come in From the Rain, Love Will Keep Us Together*.

THE CARPENTERS

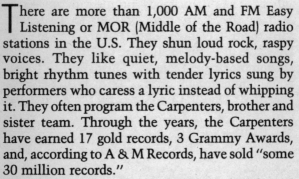

There are more than 1,000 AM and FM Easy Listening or MOR (Middle of the Road) radio stations in the U.S. They shun loud rock, raspy voices. They like quiet, melody-based songs, bright rhythm tunes with tender lyrics sung by performers who caress a lyric instead of whipping it. They often program the Carpenters, brother and sister team. Through the years, the Carpenters have earned 17 gold records, 3 Grammy Awards, and, according to A & M Records, have sold "some 30 million records."

In 1978, Karen and Richard Carpenter celebrated their 10th anniversary as recording personalities with one label, A & M. Karen plays drums and sings. Richard plays piano and sings. An early publicity shot pictures them as young people you'd meet at a high school affair. He had a kind of soup-bowl haircut, and she looked the clean-scrubbed teenager with a pretty ribbon in her hair. All in all, a portrait of a wholesome show biz team. Today they're still in the music business, even though people years ago said that their melodic style would "never sell."

Karen, 5'4", brown-eyed, was born Mar. 2, 1950. Richard, 6', hazel-eyed, was born Oct. 15, 1946. Originally, the Carpenters were from New Haven, Connecticut. Rich took accordion lessons as a boy. Later he played piano in a high school orchestra. The family moved to California, where they both attended California State College. When Karen started on drums, Rich found a bass-playing friend and they formed the Carpenter Trio, winning a Hollywood Bowl "band battle" contest in 1966, and a record contract. Later the trio broke up. The bassist moved on to play tuba with an opera company and the Carpenters went rock and formed a sextet called Spectrum, which also broke up in 1968. In 1969 A & M Records signed the Carpenters for an LP, *The Carpenters*.

They are known for their sparkling harmonies and clear, clean singing. In 1970 they had a very big year with a number-one smash, "Close to You," which still gets a lot of play. Also, they won an Oscar for Best Song of the Year — "For All We Know." In 1971 they acquired a Grammy for "Close to You." TV producers who watch the best-seller charts quickly asked them to host and star in a summer series, *Make Your Own Kind of Music*, which debuted on NBC-TV July 6, 1971.

In '72 the Carpenters were on the charts again with "Goodbye to Love" and the million-selling gold record, "Hurting Each Other," and a gold LP, *A Song for You*. In 1973 they continued a hot streak with another gold record, *Now and Then*, a number-one album. At the end of '73, they also had a million-selling single, "Top of the World." In '78 they released an ambitious collection of Christmas songs, *Christmas Portrait*. Not as big as they used to be, the Carpenters are still brand names in American pop.

SHAUN CASSIDY

In the fall of '78 there were three top teen idols —
Andy Gibb, John Travolta, and Shaun Cassidy.
Since 1976 Shaun has been a top-selling artist on
Warner Bros. Records, a TV star, and a concert
attraction. "I am a teen idol for the moment —
it's harmless," he says. "The idea of entertaining
people is fun. I take the work seriously. But I don't
take the hoopla seriously."

Born Sept. 27, 1959. Father, the late Jack Cassidy, singer-musical comedy actor. Mother, the
singer-actress, Shirley Jones. He grew up in New
York and in California in an atmosphere of show
business. His older half-brother, David, was a teen
idol too. Shaun also has two younger brothers,
Patrick and Ryan. When he was only six months
old Shaun was traveling on the road with his parents. He appeared briefly in musicals at the age
of 11. His parents tried to get Shaun interested in
his schoolwork, but without too much success.

Sometimes Shaun would go to the TV studio to
watch his mother and brother act in *The Partridge*

Family. He even asked his mother to put him in shows but she said no. At 14 Shaun formed a rock band, The Longfellow (three boys and a girl). At 16 he helped put on a show that used girl dancers. He was graduated from Beverly Hills High School but did not go on to college.

Guided by advisors, Shaun decided to go into pop music seriously. Since the U.S. is so crowded with rock newcomers, he decided to try to break through first in Germany. His first records appeared there, backed up by personal appearances. His first hit single was "Morning Girl" in 1976. Later, The Shaun Cassidy boom spread to the U.S. His first album, *Shaun Cassidy,* was the first debut album to be certified triple platinum (3 million) by the RIAA (Record Industry Association of America).

Shaun plays piano, guitar, writes songs, sings. Not long ago, *Record World* wrote: "His third album points to a maturity as a song stylist." That he is a song stylist is something of a journalistic hype. Shaun is a clean-cut, thoughtful-looking All-American pop phenomenon that girls go crazy over. That kind of magical personal appeal he has. But he is a weak singer with a thin voice (I know I'll get letters).

He isn't too happy about the exploitation angles concerning himself. "There are posters and stuff. If I had total control over merchandising, I wouldn't do any. It's kind of a cheap shot. It exploits the kids. But when the TV show started, Universal said, 'Do you want the money for these things (posters, T-shirts, lunch boxes, etc.) or we'll take it?' They'll do it either way."

Honey-colored hair with brown eyes and a small nose, Shaun is on the thin side. Athletic, he likes to play baseball and to bowl. He is close to his family. His brother David has been through the same teen-hype fame bit as he is going through now.

His career has been assisted by fantastic fan magazine coverage and the TV shows *The Hardy Boys* and *Breaking Away*. In 1979 he starred in a touching TV play about two retarded young people who marry in spite of the doubts and fears of their friends *(A Very Special Love)*.

HARRY CHAPIN

Where are the folk singers of yesteryear? The band of 20th-century troubadours with guitars who sang children's songs, songs of brotherhood, peace, and the simple life. Grizzled Pete Seger is still at it. So is Tom Paxton, and many others who keep the American tradition alive as amateur singers, songwriters, and as audience. Another member of that club is Harry Chapin. He has a modern eye, and he uses modern images to depict our times, but he still draws his inspiration from the roots of folk music. The Elektra artist is one of the most gifted of the mod folk/rock personalities.

Harry Chapin is, as *Aquarian Weekly* put it, "a citizen, singer, and a practicing Idealist." He spends practically 12 months of the year on the road doing 200 gigs; half are benefits. In 1977–78 he raised close to a million dollars for various causes. As an artist he has, through the years, acquired a gold album, a gold single, an Oscar nomination, and two Grammy nominations. One of his most touching singles is about a disc jockey writing to his wife as he takes various jobs, called "Station WORL."

He has a pleasing voice, plays guitar. Musically, he sometimes mixes folklike strains with jazz, gospel, and pop *(Living Room Suite)*. He believes everybody has to pitch in to make society work. "Anybody who is sitting on his ass and not involved in this participatory democracy is," he says, "taking a free ride." This pop activist was co-founder of the World Hunger Year in 1978. He also raises funds for the Performing Arts Foundation which aids theater, and PAF Playhouse, Huntington, L.I., which puts on productions in the schools.

Born Dec. 7, 1942, in New York's Greenwich Village. Father is a drummer, formerly with the Tommy Dorsey Orchestra and the Woody Herman swing band.

Harry started with the trumpet, then switched to guitar, playing folk music during his college years at the Air Force Academy and Cornell University. In 1964 he left school to join his brothers Tom and Steve, and their father, Jim, in a group called the Chapin Brothers. During the next few years Harry labored in films as editor and filmmaker. He made several documentaries including one that won an Academy Award nomination in 1969, *Legendary Champions* (with Jim Jacobs).

In 1971 Harry formed a group of his own, and rented the Village Gate to showcase his talent. That led to a recording contract. In 1971 he cut his first hit, "Taxi." His first solo LP was *Heads and Tales*, mostly made up of "story-songs."

There followed other LPs accenting story ballads, including a gold single, "Cat's Cradle." In 1975 Harry went to Broadway with a show, *The Night That Made America Famous*, a multi-media concept show that received two Tony nominations. In 1977 *Chapin*, a revue, ran seven months at the Improvisation Theater in Hollywood.

On LP: *Sniper and Other Love Songs, Short Stories, Verities and Balderdash* (gold record), *Portrait Gallery, Greatest Stories-Live, One the Road to Kingdom Come, Dance Band on the Titanic, Living Room Suite.*

RAY CHARLES

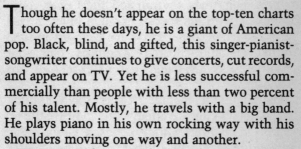

Though he doesn't appear on the top-ten charts too often these days, he is a giant of American pop. Black, blind, and gifted, this singer-pianist-songwriter continues to give concerts, cut records, and appear on TV. Yet he is less successful commercially than people with less than two percent of his talent. Mostly, he travels with a big band. He plays piano in his own rocking way with his shoulders moving one way and another.

His way with a song is very dramatic, full of changes. First he may start conversationally, then quicken the tempo, then sort of give it a blues stutter, hit the low notes, then reach up for gospelish high notes. As *The New York Times* wrote in a concert review, "Mr. Charles, like Muhammed Ali, is still the greatest."

Charles doesn't limit himself to one type of music. He does material from blues to Broadway, from soul to pop. He once declared at a concert at Carnegie Hall, "Now we're going to play what we call some true American music." And he proceeded to sing Irving Berlin's "Alexander's Rag-time Band," Rodgers and Hammerstein's "Oh, What a Beautiful Morning," and country music, as well as rhythm and blues.

He was blinded by glaucoma at six. He has managed to "overcome" and become an internationally known singer-pianist-songwriter. He was born Sept. 23, 1930, in Albany, Georgia. His full name is Ray Charles Robinson. His mother worked in a lumber mill and his father was a mechanic. He learned to read Braille and play music in the St. Augustine School for the Blind in Florida.

Wearing black glasses when he works, he interprets pop tunes, rhythm and blues, even country music with his special brand of blues, mixed with a touch of gospel. He won a Grammy in 1953 for his version of "Busted," a country song about poverty. Ray Charles currently records for Atlantic.

His singles hits include: "Georgia on My Mind" (a classic), "I Got a Woman," and "Hit the Road, Jack." On LP: *Ray Charles in Person, Genius Plus Soul, Plus Jazz, Yes Indeed, The Ray Charles Story, Love, Country Style, The Best of Ray Charles, Genius, Come Live with Me, Renaissance.*

CHIC

★

"It's very surprising to us," says bass player-singer Bernard Edwards." "Us" is Chic, one of the hottest disco acts. The group which he and guitarist Nile Rodgers formed in 1977, have already come up with two fantastically selling albums, and a multi-million selling single, "Le Freak" on Atlantic Records. In looks they resemble the upwardly mobile black middle class now making their way up the American social and economic ladder. They look very Saks Fifth Avenue "chic," which the dictionary defines as "cleverly stylish . . . currently fashionable." Quite a break away from the rock chic of blue jeans and tie-dyed T-shirts.

Chic broke into the public eye with "Dance, Dance, Dance (Yowsah, Yowsah, Yowsah)" in September 1977. It came out in two forms: a 7-inch single, and then as a 12-inch disco disc LP. *Record World* called it "one of the most perfectly elegant dance records of the year." But it was the single, "Le Freak" with its insinuating dance rhythms

that put them over. The single pushed the Bee Gees from a number-one spot. Today, Chic is riding the crest of the disco boom, with recordings and personal appearances. *Variety* describes them as "one of the better disco bands, especially in their offbeat string section and in the vocal department."

Bernard Edwards says, "We're trying to establish an entertaining kind of music. We're not trying to deliver any heavy message, just entertainment. When you're off from work, come and see us and have a good time and split—that's it."

The co-founder of Chic was born in Greenville, North Carolina, came to New York at 10, joined the P.S. 164 recorder band in Brooklyn, then learned tenor saxophone in junior high. Later he went on to New York's High School of Performing Arts, where he switched from horns to electric bass. His partner, Nile, was born on the Triborough Bridge en route to Queens General Hospital (Queens, N.Y.) and once worked in the Apollo house band and also on TV's *Sesame Street*. In 1972 he and Bernard formed the Big Apple Band that acted as a backup band for a rock group called New York City. The unit broke up in 1975.

In 1977 they got busy again to produce "Everybody Dance." In June '77 they coined the new name, Chic. There have been changes, people coming in and out of the group since. At this writing, Chic key figures include drummer Tommy Thompson, lead singer Alfa Anderson, and singer Luci Martin.

Chic is now a brand name in the field of disco, as a recording and touring group. To take care of business, there's even a management firm with a fancy name: The Chic Organization, Ltd.

At the same time, the two founders, Bernard and Nile, have produced and written songs for an album by a Cotillion group, Sister Sledge, who are coming up.

Chic singles: "Dance, Dance, Dance," "Everybody Dance," and "Le Freak." On LP: *Chic, C'est Chic*.

CHICAGO

Not long ago, Chicago was down in Miami's Criteria Studio at the request of the Bee Gees. The Bee Gees wanted a brass sound in their new LP, *Spirits Having Flown*. So they asked Chicago to sit in and provide the special horn flavor for which they're famous.

Chicago is a top jazz-rock group that has its musical roots in the big swing bands of the 1940s. It started on the campus of De Paul University in Chicago. Later, the group moved to Los Angeles. Says Walt Parazaider, who plays woodwinds: "We left Chicago like migrant farmers. Drove 36 hours straight. It was like Laurel and Hardy. We even tore the door off the car, backing up and forgetting to shut it."

When they reached Los Angeles in the late sixties, they practiced seven days a week, with eight-hour-a-day rehearsal sessions. Their first modest hit was "Make Me Smile." Since then they have emerged as one of the top rock groups. Today they function as an eight-man group: Peter Cetera, bass; Donnie Dacus, guitar; Laudir de Oliveira, percussion; Robert Lamm, keyboards; Lee Loughnane, trumpet; Walt Parazaider; James Pankov, trombone; and Danny Seraphine, drums.

Their sales stats are fantastic. According to Columbia, each of Chicago's eleven albums (so far) have reached platinum status. The group's albums have sold to 20 million people, generating $160 million in sales. In concerts they are equally hot. Their 1977 European tour was a smash and so was a swing through the U.S. in 1978.

Chicago has turned to show biz, with some doubtful results. At the Greek Theatre in Los Angeles not too long ago, Chicago added a big 40-member string section, what *Variety* called "a lush touch." Also, they performed with a glittering art deco set. Later on, the Los Angeles Ballet danced to a medley of Chicago's "greatest hits." While sets, dance, and string sections can often add to a presentation, it depends on whether they fit the band's musical style.

There is no "star" in this band. All are excellent musicians. One critic, Robert Gold, writing in the *Los Angeles Free Press*, called them the "most inventive, hardest blowing jazz-rock orchestra I have ever heard." He added that "the singing is sweet as well as wild" and that the "ensemble horn playing is phenomenal, creative, rhythmic, colorful, bold."

Chicago started out as an innovative group. "You have to remember," says Lee Loughnane, "we were heavy FM. Long songs, complicated arrangements." "Make Me Smile" ran 12 minutes. They still try new things. All kinds of influences filter into the evolving Chicago sound. Jazz, classical, rock, Latin. Their new percussionist, Laudir de Oliveira, who used to be with Sergio Mendes, has added "a silky afterbeat" from cool Latin jazz.

Chicago single hits: "Baby What a Big Surprise," "Wishing You Were Here," and "Feeling Stronger Every Day." Most of their LPs have numbered titles, *Chicago I, Chicago II, Chicago III*, etc. After *Chicago XI* they apparently got tired of counting and switched to something new, and called a 1978 album *Hot Streets*. One other non-numbered LP is called *Chicago at Carnegie Hall*.

ERIC CLAPTON

More than 10 years ago, a jokester in a British rock club watched Eric Clapton's fingers racing on the guitar. Eric's hands were a blur. As a gag, an absurd gag, he nicknamed him "Slowhand." That nickname stuck, and still later became the title of a successful hit album on RSO Records.

"Slowhand" Eric Clapton, an ace guitarist, is one of the mainstays of rock. Now on his own, and functioning under his own name, he has worked with Cream, John Mayall's Bluesbreakers, Derek and the Dominos, and Blind Faith. He is an example of the rock musician who goes in and out of rock groups like a revolving door. He's also a classic example of the rock musician as an instrumental star rather than a vocalist.

With the guitar so dominant in rock, Eric is a glamour figure. He is to contemporary pop what Segovia is to classical guitar. His fingers move over the strings and the frets with great intensity and feeling. Eric performs hard rock, his own versions of oldtime blues, even country and western songs. Through the years he has topped many music polls as "top guitarist." In the 1979 *Playboy* music poll, the veteran once again headed the list of guitar pickers: Eric Clapton, Carlos Santana, Joe Walsh, Jimmy Page, and Ted Nugent.

Born in England Mar. 30, 1945. He's 5'11", and has brown eyes and carefully trimmed sideburns and mustache. He's the son of a Surrey bricklayer named John Clapp. At one time, he thought he wanted to be a stained glass window designer. But he discovered the guitar and that's become his whole world. He puts down those who say he's the best guitarist in the world. "That's ridiculous," he states.

In the late seventies Clapton signed with RSO Records, the pop conglomerate run by Robert Stigwood, whose other recording artists include the Bee Gees and Andy Gibb. Eric is also starting to write a lot. For the LP *Slowhand*, he wrote five new songs on his own, and with collaborators. One of them was a gentle ballad about his current girl friend, named Patti, called "Wonderful Tonight." That girl happened to be Patti Boyd, formerly married to ex-Beatle George Harrison. On March 27, 1979, Clapton wed her while on tour in Tucson, Arizona. To avoid publicity the two exchanged vows in an out-of-the-way church in a Mexican-American neighborhood. Patti wore a lace dress and Eric shone in a sparkling white tuxedo.

While on a solo kick, Eric often sits in as a studio musician for other rock groups and rock stars like Pete Townsend of The Who. He could get all the work he wants if he wanted to free-lance, but that way he loses a lot of money. In 1977 Eric and his new band raced around giving concerts all over Europe. He even went to engagements aboard the famed *Orient Express*. That same year he also appeared in Japan and Hawaii. In Hawaii he was joined onstage by Yvonne Elliman. In 1978 he also made a tour of the USA, followed by dates all over Latin America. In 1979 he found the American Southwest.

After years of living in the Bahamas, Clapton now lives in England once more. A man with an offbeat sense of humor, he likes odd pictures of animals such as one showing a fiddling dog. He hung that one on his bathroom wall.

Clapton on LP: *Slowhand, Backless.*

★
JUDY COLLINS
★

Singer, pianist, guitarist, actress, activist, composer, filmmaker. They all come together in
5'5" Judy Collins. Born in Seattle, May 1, 1939,
she started taking piano lessons at age 5. Her father
was a West Coast radio personality, Chuck Collins. As a youngster her family moved to Denver.
At 13 Judy was featured in a concert in which she
played Mozart's "Concerto for Two Pianos."

In the fifties she was attracted to folk music.
But not folk music only in the old vintage manner
but mod folk songs with contemporary and poetic
lyrics and new tunes. She appeared in local folk
clubs around Denver, where she impressed people
with her cool, clear, pure voice, her polished,
knowing musicality. Unlike most folk singers, she
could read music.

A small record company in the East just starting
out, Elektra, heard of her and signed her up. Two
of her early LPs were *Maid of Constant Sorrow*
and *Golden Apples of the Sun*. These won a lot
of praise. *Time* magazine wrote that she was a
"major contender for the female folk crown,"
along with Joan Baez.

Slim, with blue-gray eyes, Judy has discovered many new songs and songwriters. She heard a haunting song by poet Leonard Cohen and turned it into a hit, "Suzanne." She also hit the charts with one of Joni Mitchell's best compositions, a thoughtful song called "Both Sides Now."

Open to all sorts of influences, Judy Collins defies labeling. Along with folk and contemporary folk, she has also recorded material from musical theater. She has done such unusual numbers as "Marat Sade," about two famed figures in the French Revolution, and songs by Kurt Weill and Bertold Brecht. In the early seventies she cut a top-ten single, the touching "Send In the Clowns," from the Broadway musical, *A Little Night Music.* It was the first show tune in a long time to reach the top-ten.

An activist, she lends her name to causes and even performs to raise money for specific projects. In 1964 she went to Mississippi to help with the registration of black voters. In 1967 she worked with the Women's Strike for Peace. She also co-produced an LP called *Save the Children* for needy children.

On the personal side, she enjoys skiing, Thomas Hardy, and the legend of Joan of Arc. Recently, she's turned to filmmaking (one about a woman conductor) and songwriting. She wrote two songs for the album *Wildflowers:* "Since You Asked Me" and "Albatross." She has had five gold records on Elektra, among them *Wildflowers, In My Life, Who Knows Where the Time Goes, Whales and Nightingales, Colors of the Day,* and *Judith.*

THE COMMODORES

Motown, which has guided the Supremes, the Temptations, and the Jacksons, has specialized in building black pop groups. It does it with a high concentration of purpose, road tours, and heavy disc jockey promotion. Sometimes it launches a group, nothing happens, and the group is quickly dropped. Sometimes it launches a group, and patiently waits for something to happen. It took almost eight years for the Commodores to really happen. The Commodores are a seven-member instrumental and vocal group. The members are Ronald LaPread, Lionel Richie, Thomas McClary, Milan Williams, Walter Orange, Bennie Ashburn, and William King.

Billboard once reviewed *Commodores' Greatest Hits* and wrote: "This soul outfit has become a major attraction because of a gifted ability to combine soul and pop elements which appeal to a wide cross section of fans. Here they remind everyone of their unique style with a mix of ballads and up-tempo tunes that both caress and boogie." Their vocal efforts are backed with "sassy orchestrations."

The combo started in the South. Years ago when they were college students they were known as The Jays. In 1968 they left Alabama's famed Tuskegee Institute and set out to crack the music business in New York. Instead of hitting it big and becoming rich overnight, they found themselves unable to eat and pay the rent. For the next few years they performed summers in Europe and Canada, while continuing their education at Tuskegee. The highlight of their summers away was a shipboard performance on the S.S. *France*. It was reportedly "a first." The first time any black rock group was employed to entertain on a luxury liner catering mostly to white passengers.

In 1970 they signed up with Motown Records. The company remembered the shipboard concerts and changed their name to the Commodores. As a first step in a build-up, they became the first act to tour with The Jackson Five. The Commodores' first album for Motown was *Machine Gun*.

In 1978 it had one of the top smashes, the number-one single in America, "Three Times a Lady." That single can be found in their album, *Natural High*. Motown has reported that the LP has sold more than 3 million copies (records and tapes). It's what the trade press calls a "triple platinum album." During the summer of '78, the Commodores outsold John Travolta, Olivia Newton-John, Andy Gibb, and the Rolling Stones, so far as singles were concerned.

Two years ago they picked up *Billboard's* Talent in Action Award as Top Soul Album Artists, and the Top Box Office Artists playing arenas from six to 20 thousand.

For "Three Times a Lady," the Commodores received a special ASCAP award. Other hits by this down-home group are: "Brick House," "Easy" and "Machine Gun." Other Motown albums: *Live, Natural High.*

RITA COOLIDGE

A star on her own, she has also appeared in sell-out concerts with her former husband, Kris Kristofferson. She's a singer, pianist, bandleader. Born in Nashville, Tennessee, in 1944. Her voice has been described as having "a smoky Southern tone." Her route to stardom came via backup vocals.

Willowy, she has long hair which she parts down the middle. She looks slightly American Indian, and she is. Her roots are Cherokee Indian and Southern white. Her father was a Baptist minister. Being of church people, Rita found herself singing church hymns. Later she got to know country music and rhythm and blues, which comes pouring out of Nashville radio. She and her sister, Priscilla, began performing in school during her teen years. In the early seventies, it was her sister who broke through first, recording with Booker T of Stax Records.

One thing led to another, and soon Rita was asked to sing backup vocals for another Stax group,

Delaney and Bonnie Bramlett. When the D & B unit went on the road, they took Rita with them. Soon her name got around. It is reported that Leon Russell wrote a hit song, "Delta Lady," as a salute to her. Rita continued her backup career with Leon Russell and Joe Cocker. On tours with the aggregation of Russell and Cocker Mad Dogs and Englishmen, Rita got to sing a song by herself, stage center, called "Superstar." After that, she added to her earnings by working steadily as a backup singer at record sessions for other artists. Sometimes she played piano too.

In 1970 A & M Records signed Rita. In 1971 they released her first LP, simply titled *Rita Coolidge*. It was well received. Her songs were penned by a diverse number of pop names—Neil Young, Van Morrison, and Smokey Robinson.

Now a wife and a mother of one daughter, Rita lives in Malibu, California. She continues to be active not only in recordings and concerts, but also as a guest star on leading TV shows.

Rita's gold record singles: "Higher and Higher," "We're All Alone." On LP: *Anytime*.

NATALIE COLE

Radio stations play "golden oldies" but, unfortunately, a lot of them don't play Nat "King" Cole. In the fifties he was a great singer of ballads and a pianist with the lightly swinging jazz group, the Nat "King" Cole Trio. His daughter is 5'10" Natalie Cole, a Capitol Records recording star.

As a kid, she grew up in Los Angeles. She remembers the biggest names in music coming to visit: Pearl Bailey, Nancy Wilson, Ella Fitzgerald, Sarah Vaughn, and Count Basie.

"I was very friendly and gave tours of our home," she recalls. "I talked too much. I was a ham, a very independent child. I wasn't spoiled, just full of energy."

The model-slim singer went to private schools. As a youngster she played piano in a group that included the sons of conductor Carmen Dragon and Nelson Riddle, the famed arranger for Sinatra and others. In 1966 her father died of cancer.

In 1968 she went to the University of Massachusetts, planning to become a child psychologist. There she got involved with anti-war activity, and the civil rights movement. She joined a rock group that performed on weekends. She wore hot pants, boots, the wig—the whole rock chic shtick. Anyway, she dropped the idea of child psychology as a career to pursue pop music. Her career wasn't all upward and onward. Once she got a job in Las Vegas, only to bomb badly.

Her first album, *Inseparable*, was released in 1975. In 1976 Natalie won two Grammys as New Artist of the Year and another, Best R & R Female Vocal Performance, for her hit single, "This Will Be." She's also had a TV special of her own, and she's had a successful one-woman concert produced at the Metropolitan Opera House in Lincoln Center in 1978. In a review of that concert, the *New York Post* wrote: "In just over three years, Natalie Cole has accomplished the impossible: She has developed a singing personna of her own."

"Natalie," wrote *Ebony* [May 1978] is her own woman, a musical phenomenon who exploded on the national scene three short years ago, rising to the top like cream with a dazzling touch of versatility: ballads, torch-rock, rhythm and blues."

She has a three-year-old son, Robert Adam. She is presently separated from her husband, a songwriter-record producer, Marvin Yancy, who has assisted her in making personal appearances and records. The future looks bright for the daughter of a great pop star. She goes her own musical way (less sophisticated material, more funky, black-oriented songs), but she remembers her father. At the end of "The Natalie Cole Special" on TV, she did a medley of his hits ("Mona Lisa," etc.), with tears streaming down her face.

Natalie Cole discs include *Unpredictable* (platinum record), *Thankful*, *Natalie . . . Live* (double LP set).

ELVIS COSTELLO

There's another Elvis in pop—Elvis Costello. He has a long, triangular face, long forehead, and he wears big horn-rimmed glasses. He has a tendency to wear shirts of any size (thrift store specials). His trousers are generally straight leg, almost pegged, hugging the ankles. He performs almost in a comical knock-kneed fashion. He's an intelligent sort of a punk rocker who's got a lot to say.

Costello, a Columbia Records star, is a feverish rocker from Great Britain. His songs are thoughtful. They deal with power in human relationships, with commercialism, with the problems of monotonous work. There's a lot of anger in him. Take his song, "Radio Radio," that attacks the Top-40 formula:

> The radio's in the hands
>   Of such a lot of fools
> Trying to anesthesize
> The way you feel

He did this on *Saturday Night Live*. Another theme of his is the way plain people try to dom-

inate each other, "Two Hitlers." Elvis (his first name is from you know who) also has a way with words. In one song he describes one girl this way: "Her mouth is made up but her mind is undone."

Newsweek, *The Village Voice*, and *The New York Times* have all praised Costello as a biting songwriter and as a powerhouse performer. His music is mostly fifties and sixties rock, sometimes flavored with a little Caribbean reggae. On stage, he often acts as if he is in terrible pain. "People," wrote one critic in *Phonograph Records* (Jan. 1978), "are already talking about the legendary qualities of his performances."

His real name is Declan Patrick McManus. His father, a jazz trumpeter and singer, deserted his family. He left Elvis (and his mother) when he was a young child. Elvis grew up in a working-class neighborhood in London and took up the guitar as a teenager. At 18 he worked at computers. At the same time he got weekend jobs as a guitarist with pickup bands. His first album was *My Aim Is True* on Stiff Records. In July 1977 Columbia Records officials were in London and Elvis, the story goes, rushed over and gave an open-air audition in the street outside the hotel.

His home is in Acton, England. He has a four-year-old son. Among his own favorite artists are Joni Mitchell and David Bowie. In 1979 he had a smash top-ten album, *Armed Forces*, which is about combat of all types. His singles include: "This Year's Girl" (an attack on the fashion biz), "Oliver's Army" and "Good Squad" (both anti-war), "Accidents Will Happen," and "Watching the Detectives."

JOHN DENVER

John Denver, "The Sunshine Kid." He goes on being upbeat in a jaded world, heavy with disco fever. And he continues to be successful with his gentle sunny approach. "My music," he says, "is a celebration of life, all aspects of life. Everybody is calling out how crappy life is, how hard it is. They're talking about drudgery, murder, killings. Yes, that's all out there, but it's only one side of the picture. Now look around you. There are trees, rivers, lakes, mountains. I want to tell people how great the world is."

Denver's commitment to songs praising the beauty of nature, "roots," the family, the uncomplicated life, is still as strong as ever. The singer-songwriter-guitarist-TV personality records in Los Angeles. He has cut 15 RCA albums so far, nine of them gold records, several of them platinum. His total sales (according to an RCA spokesman) are an estimated 200 million (records, tapes, cassettes). Besides the USA, he is especially popular in South Africa, Australia, Germany, and Japan.

Denver sees pop music as a commercial business hype but one that has a deeper function. He thinks that "music is not so much a form of entertainment but the life-style of a people." He's happiest when people use his songs and absorb them in their lives. That's what's happened. Students quote his lyrics at high school graduations. His songs about nature ("Rocky Mountain High") have become anthems for the ecology movement. Psychologists are keen on "Looking for Space," which is about the search for identity and the pain of self-development.

The 5'11" singer, who wears steel- and gold-rimmed glasses, is the son of one of America's most famous test pilots, Lt. Colonel Henry Deutschendorf, S. (Retired). John was born Dec. 31, 1943, in Roswell, New Mexico. He led a nomadic life as a young boy from one air base to another in the Southwest. His love affair with music began when his grandmother gave him a 1912 Gibson guitar for his tenth birthday.

His first big break came when he got a job with the Chad Mitchell Trio. It was a folk-oriented group that did socially significant material as well as satirical numbers. When rock rolled over folk, Denver went solo. In 1969 he signed with RCA. As a songwriter his first big hit was "Leaving on a Jet Plane." He loves to perform, be in front of audiences, whether it be a "freebie" for kids or in Las Vegas with Frank Sinatra.

John's home is in Aspen, Colorado. He lives with his wife, Annie, and his two adopted children, Zachary John, 5, and Anna Kate, 3. He skis, backpacks, does do-it-yourself projects, rides a motorcycle, goes to the movies. Incidentally, he's a movie actor too. He starred in the hit, *Oh, God*.

A tenor with power, John has an easy way with an audience. His material is slightly down-home, slightly country, slightly rock, slightly middle-of-the-road. Among his albums are: *Windsong, Spirit*, and *John Denver*. His biggest selling album so far has been *John Denver's Greatest Hits*, selling six million copies. It contains such favorites as "Leaving on a Jet Plane," "Follow Me," "Back Home," "Thank God I'm a Country Boy," and "Windsong."

NEIL DIAMOND

His parents owned a dry-goods store in Brighton Beach, Brooklyn, New York, a folksy neighborhood that borders the Atlantic Ocean. As a youngster, Neil (born Jan. 24, 1941) loved to listen to the radio. In his teens he formed a folk music group. He learned to imitate folk, folk-rock, and even gospel-type tunes. He was also introverted and rebellious.

After attending Lincoln High School, he enrolled as a pre-med student at NYU. He left college to break into pop music. He began writing songs on a guitar and, with contacts from the old neighborhood, started making the rounds. In the mid-sixties he got a job writing songs for about $50 a week with a Tin Pan Alley music publisher.

"What I was writing were specific songs for specific people. Someone would be coming up for a session, so I would write a song like his last hit," he once told BMI's *World of Music*.

The black-haired, intense, singer-songwriter had many of his songs recorded by leading artists and groups. He stepped out as a solo performer on Bang Records. At his first studio session, he cut three hits, "Solitary Man," "Cherry Cherry," and "I Got a Feeling." Later he switched to UNI (later renamed MCA). During five years there (1967–1972) he produced eight albums, all gold records. Wooed by a big money deal he moved to Columbia. His first Columbia release in 1974 was a multi-million selling soundtrack album of the film, *Jonathan Livingston Seagull*, for which Neil wrote the score.

Moody, he is a hard worker. In 1970 he had a number-one hit, a gold record, "Cracklin' Rose," on UNI. His songwriting hits include "Sunday and Me," and "I'm a Believer" (for the Monkees). A few years ago he departed from his soft ballads rock style to take a flier, linking rock with African rock songs in an LP, *Tap Root Manuscript*.

In 1972 Diamond, tired of "the road," retired from active performing. He wanted to spend "more time with his family." In 1976 he returned with personal appearances in Australia and New Zealand. That same year he earned $500,000 in three concerts in Las Vegas.

Now living on the West Coast, Diamond continues to write, study music, and perform. In 1977 he starred in a TV special, NBC's "I'm Glad You're Here with Me."

Time has described his musical approach this way: "Diamond long ago found a formula that really works: sentimental lyrics, sing-along tunes, jagged rhythms." Lately he's been experimenting with all sorts of arranging patterns, even using lashing saxes and lush strings. In '79 he had a number-one singles hit, a duet with Barbra Streisand (also a former Brooklynite), "You Don't Bring Me Flowers."

On LP: *Love at the Greek* (double record), *Hot August Night* (more than eight million copies sold world-wide), and *Beautiful Noise* (covering his Tin Pan Alley days).

THE DOOBIE
BROTHERS

★

The Doobie Brothers aren't brothers. And they did not originate the scat phrase, "doobie-do." But they are a top West Coast rock instrumental and vocal group. *Blast* magazine, put out by DIR Broadcasting, syndicators of rock programs, once said that "the group has consistently recorded some of the most interesting rock of the 1970s."

Like most of today's rock bands they are a mix; a blend of rock, blues, "soul," country. "We don't judge our music, it's tough for us to," John Hartman, a founding member once stated. "We usually leave it up to the listeners. If it does well, we get comments from radio stations and newspapers, and then we have a general idea of how we've done."

Successful through the years, without too much hype, the Doobie Brothers scored a stunning double triumph in March '79. Their album, *Minute*

by Minute (largely about love) reached the number-one spot on the best-seller charts. At the same time, a single cut from the LP, "What a Fool Believes" reached number one on the singles charts. In a frantic field where about 80 percent of records produced do not sell enough to pay back production costs, this was quite an achievement, and made Warner Brothers very happy.

The California band was organized in San Jose in 1969. Its early members were Tom Johnston (lead singer/guitarist), Skip Spencer (guitar), Gregg Murphy (bass), John Hartman (drummer). Through the years it added and subtracted members. They got their act together playing clubs in Northern California, around San Francisco. A demo tape caught the interest of Warner Bros. Records. Their first LP, *The Doobie Brothers*, came out in 1971. Few sales, but good reviews. In 1972 they scored with a single, "Listen to the Music." Since then they have made vinyl waves with a series of best-selling singles and albums, including "The Captain and Me" and "What Were Once Vices Are Now Habits."

In '79 the band itself announced "with regret" that John Hartman and Jeff ("Skunk") Baxter had dropped out. Nobody seemed to know why. Remaining are Michael McDonald, Patrick Simmons, Tiran Porter, and Keith Knudsen, none from the original band.

They have a unique style of writing. "Usually what we start with is an instrumental track with no vocals," says Micahel McDonald. "The words will probably go along with what the music feels like. The band writes more from a musician's standpoint than someone like Kris Kristofferson, who writes a story idea and then writes the music around that. We usually write lyrics around our music."

In February 1977 Dinah Shore saluted the band on her syndicated show with a 90-minute "Visit With The Doobies." In January '78 the Doobie Brothers appeared in a two-part episode of the ABC-TV sitcom, *What's Happening!*

The band has lent their name and talent to raise money for worthwhile charities, such as a golf tournament, The Doobie Brothers Golf Classic, and the Concert for the United Way. Then there's the annual Doobie Brothers Christmas party at the Children's Hospital at Stanford University in Palo Alto, California. The hospital treats seriously ill and handicapped children from 11 western states. The Doobie Brothers perform and give away records and stockings packed with gifts. The band has also aided a non-profit theater group, Theatricum Botanicum, organized by the late Will Geer, who was a star on *The Waltons*.

Doobie Brothers on LP: *Stampede, Takin' It to the Streets, Best of the Doobies, Livin' on the Fault Line* (all gold and platinum). *The Best of the Doobies* has sold more than three million (records, tapes, etc.), triple platinum.

★
BOB DYLAN
★

Wiry Bob Dylan continues to write songs, cut records, make appearances, and fool around with films. However, he is not the giant of pop music he used to be in terms of popular appeal. His recent TV specials, including *Hard Rain* on NBC, were poorly received, and his try at a feature film, *Renaldo and Clara*, was a fizzle. Complicated, he's a pop millionaire who still looks at life from the standpoint of a grim outsider. Separated, he is the father of five children.

The world of folk music, of protest songs, of "hoots," gave birth to Dylan. Through the years he has produced a body of work as a singer-songwriter that still stands as a chunk of American cultural history. Students and writers still quote from his songs such as "Blowin' in the Wind," "The Times They Are A-Changing'," and "Gods of War." His success helped put over several ideas that revolutionized the record business and popular music: that strong controversial material could sell, that artists could pick what to record rather than some company record-producer who's trying to be "commercial," the radio stations would play controversial songs and the world wouldn't fall down, and that modern poetry techniques could be used in writing popular songs.

Owner of a raspy voice, Dylan's singing style is close to his oldtime idol, Woody Guthrie. He plays the guitar and harmonica efficiently. He has limited composing skills. Most of his tunes sound like traditional folk songs, or country songs, mixed with the blues and some rock. His ideas and his language are his strong suit.

In his biography, *On Record*, the man who discovered him, John Hammond, pointed out that Dylan "with persistence and intensity opposed war profiteers, lynchers, racists, and all forms of injustice"; also, that Dylan was a superlative artist who could take personal experiences and turn them into "dramatic poetry."

Singer-songwriter-musician Bob Dylan was born Robert Zimmerman in Duluth, Minnesota, May 24, 1941, of Jewish parents. Once strongly political, he has since turned increasingly personal. He's down on today's politics. He once told *TV Guide*, "I'd like to see Thomas Jefferson, Benjamin Franklin, and a few other guys come back. They knew what was happening."

In that interview, he was asked what he liked to read. He replied he read a lot of Artur Rimbaud, the French mystical poet, and novelist Herman Melville. "Yes, Rimbaud has been a big influence on me. When I'm on the road and want to read something that makes sense to me I go to a bookshop and read his words. Melville is somebody I can identify with because of how he looked at life. I also like Joseph Conrad a lot and I've loved what I've read of James Joyce. Allen Ginsberg is always a great inspiration.''

Dylan on LP: *Bob Dylan, Blonde on Blonde, Highway 16 Revisited, Nashville Skyline, Street Legal.*

THE EAGLES

The Grammy Awards are getting to resemble the Oscars. From time to time pop stars and groups decide not to attend for one reason or another. In 1978 one pop group decided to boycott the event because it felt that it wouldn't win anyway. This happened to the Eagles, an "anti-award" cocky California band. Only what happened is that they did win. Their album *Hotel California* was named "Record of the Year."

According to the *Hit Parader*, "touring is what built the Eagles into what they are today." Their singles hits include "Best of My Love," "James Dean," and "Lyin' Eyes" (about marriage problems). In 1978 it was such a hot rock group that there was an ad in *Billboard* that went:

A MILLION A MONTH
FOR THE PAST 18 MONTHS, THE EAGLES
HAVE SOLD 1 MILLION
ALBUMS EVERY 30 DAYS

The West Coast band has been on a hot streak. Several years ago the *Eagles' Greatest Hits* LP was on the charts for almost 100 weeks, and sold more than seven million. And in 1978 their *Hotel California* proved to be a monster seller. More than nine million copies were sold worldwide. It was the biggest selling record of the year for Elektra/Asylum.

Eagles is mostly a "roots" band, sticking close to country-style rock and roll. However, it has also done songs with a string section backing. It's a vocal and instrumental group that's changed personnel through the years. Today its leading members are Joe Walsh (guitar, vocals); Glenn Frey (piano, guitar, vocals, harp); Don Henley (vocals, drums); Don Felder (guitar, vocals); and Timothy Schmit. It got started in the early seventies. A leading, original figure in the group, Glenn Frey began playing in high school bands and once played backup for singer Linda Ronstadt.

Asylum signed them up in 1972. Its first album was called *The Eagles*. It hit the charts and made a bit of a name for itself. Later on, the group promoted itself with a series of concert tours. Among its singles hits have been "Witchy Woman," "Take It Easy," and "Desperado."

By 1976 the group had developed quite a following, largely on the West Coast. In that year, for example, it played four sold-out concerts at the Los Angeles Forum. Despite a slow start, with too many sad songs, according to *Variety*, the pop group ended up strong.

Not long ago in an article on the music business, "The Best Comes East," in *New York* magazine, somehow the Eagles came up—and in an odd way. The president of Columbia Records, Walter Yetnikoff, was talking about the young people's attachment to pop. He added, "The most charismatic people in American culture emanate from the music business—it's the most exciting part of American culture. My kids would rather see the Eagles, or Bruce Springsteen in a movie than Redford."

Today the Eagles are flying high. Whether it will ever achieve the sales heights again as in *Hotel California* remains to be seen. Meanwhile, they continue to perform and record, under the direction of a shrewd manager, Irving Azoff.

Eagles on LP: *The Eagles, Hotel California, One of These Nights, On the Border, The Eagles' Greatest Hits.*

EARTH, WIND
AND FIRE

This group mixes showmanship, light shows, and space suits with songs of brotherhood, done in a funky style. Some of their magical tricks have been devised by Doug Henning of the famed *The Magic Show*. Behind the glitter is a message that life can provide good vibrations. And music can help us. So insists Maurice White, the main man, founder of the award-winning Columbia/Arc group.

"We live in a negative society," says Maurice. "Most people can't see beauty and love. I see our music as medicine."

If its medicine, its fans can't get enough of it. The lyrics are jazzy with a touch of Oriental meditative philosophy. The music is a blend of gospel, jazz, hard rock, and disco. That, mixed in with their live shows, which are full of gimmicks and dazzling lighting, has proved to be a potent draw.

The sales stats of Earth, Wind and Fire at the record counters are fantastic. In 1978, in an article titled, "The Power of Positive Singing," *Newsweek* reported that "each of their four last albums has sold more than two million copies." And during that same year, they went on a 70-city tour that drew an average of 16,000 fans, despite blizzard and snowy conditions along much of the tour. So far, they have earned seven gold albums, of which five are platinum, and four are double platinum; four gold singles; Grammy Awards; and American Music Awards.

A former drummer doing rhythm and blues and jazz, Maurice White, of Chicago, established Earth, Wind and Fire in 1967. It was he who developed the concept of a combo that would not only entertain but uplift the spirit. His Columbia Records bio says, "He realized that the arts can be responsible for changing the way people relate to their own problems and goals, and goals of the world at large."

This isn't all PR. Earth, Wind and Fire tries to do this. For example, there's the message of the title song of the LP, *Head to Sky*. Here is developed the concept of positive thinking to attain your goals. In another LP, *That's the Way of the World*, each of the lyrics try to point up the spiritual thoughts of the group.

The personnel of the vocal/instrumental band has changed since the early days. At first it was a jazz group, which recorded on Warner Bros. Currently its members are: Maurice White, Verdine White, Philip Bailey, Larry Dunn, Al McKay, Johnny Graham, Andrew Woolfolk, Fred White, and Ralph Johnson. They sing and they play everything from congas to kaliba (a version of an African instrument) to synthesizer to saxes.

On LP (Columbia/Arc); *Last Days and Times, Head to the Sky, Open Our Eyes, Spirit, All 'N All, Best of Earth, Wind and Fire Vol 1.* Its big singles include "Singasong," "Can't Hide Love," "Getaway," "Serpentine Fire."

★
YVONNE ELLIMAN
★

E arly in 1979 TV's detective program, *Hawaii Five-O*, did a show about the world of rock and disco in Hawaii. Playing a small but important role as a young and promising singer was Yvonne Elliman. It was good casting. Yvonne is a promising singer and is from the sun-splashed islands. Small, black-haired, and young, she has had quite a career so far, capped by a number-one hit, "If I Can't Have You."

Possessing a small-ranged but strong, sweet voice, Yvonne can sing out with a rock pulse. She left her native Hawaii when she was 17 and headed for London seeking work as a singer. Her first job was at a Kings Road club, The Pheasantry. As luck would have it, Tim Rice and Andrew Lloyd Webber, authors of *Jesus Christ Superstar*, were in the audience. Yvonne was immediately hired to play Mary Magdalene ("I Don't Know How to Love

Him"). As a member of that now legendary production, Yvonne recorded the original album, performed in major theaters throughout the world, and appeared in the film version. Her screen performance was so outstanding, the Hollywood Foreign Press Association nominated Yvonne for the Golden Globe Award as Best Actress.

While appearing in *Jesus Christ Superstar* on Broadway, Yvonne also cut her first solo LP for Decca Records. Nonetheless, believing she was losing sight of her own identity in the part of Mary Magdalene, Yvonne chose to return to London. There she recorded another solo album with help from The Who's Peter Townsend.

Yvonne returned to the U.S. just when Eric Clapton came out of his self-imposed retreat. While Clapton was recording in Miami, Yvonne went to the studio to listen to him work. Needing a strong female vocalist for the chorus in Clapton's "I Shot the Sheriff," Eric recruited Yvonne. Later, when Eric formed his band, Yvonne was the female vocalist he sought. Yvonne worked with Clapton for three years, touring and recording the albums *461 Ocean Boulevard* (co-writing "Get Ready" with Eric), *There's One in Every Crowd*, *E. C. Was Here*, *No Reason to Cry*, and (their last one together) *Slowhand*.

Although she enjoyed her years with Eric Clapton, Yvonne was determined to work solo. She signed with RSO Records and cut an LP, *Rising Sun*. It wasn't until her second RSO album, *Love Me*, that Yvonne really attracted notice as a solo artist. Two singles from *Love Me*, the title cut and "Hello Stranger," both hit the Top-20 on best-seller charts. "Hello Stranger" remained in the number one spot on MOR charts for several weeks. Her next LP, *Night Flight*, contained the smash number-one hit, "If I Can't Have You."

In 1977 Yvonne Elliman was awarded the Don Kirshner Rock Award as Best Female Vocalist. *Billboard* magazine nominated Yvonne as 1977's Top Vocalist in their Easy Listening category.

★
ROBERTA FLACK
★

She's probably one of the few in the world of pop to actually have a bachelor's degree in music education. She knows Bach as well as black soul and rock. Her academic training hasn't hurt her, since she has acquired Grammys and gold records. One of her biggest single hits was "The First Time Ever I Saw Your Face." Her voice is compelling, musical, and strong.

The gifted singer-pianist was born in Washington, D.C., Feb. 10, 1939. She studied piano at an early age. After attending high school, she went on to the famed black college, Howard University, in Washington, D.C., enrolling as a music major. After graduation, she got a job teaching school in Farmville, North Carolina, in the sixties.

"I had to work like hell from seven in the morning till seven at night," she says. "I crammed so much music down their throats you wouldn't believe it. I wanted to give them so much. They'd never sung four-part harmony together before. Or heard Bach's chorales. And the kids loved it. They'd come to rehearsal even after picking tobacco all day, when they couldn't even come to school."

More teaching followed, and then she got a job accompanying opera singers at the Tivoli Restaurant in Georgetown, a fancy section of Washington. She even helped put on a scaled-down production of *Aida* there. Later on, Roberta herself was put on stage. This led to a contract with Atlantic Records.

Musically she moves easily from soul to ballads to rock. Her first LP was *First Take* in 1969 and got on the charts. She guested on a lot of TV shows, including a Bill Cosby special. Her second LP was called *Chapter Two*.

In the early seventies she teamed up with Donny Hathaway to produce a number of best-selling singles and albums. In 1979 they were at work on a recording project when Hathaway committed suicide.

Through the years, Roberta has won four Grammys. However, in 1979 she criticized the way the Grammy Awards are structured on TV. "Why does it have to be a middle-of-the-road white hosting the program? I can read cue cards too." Also, she thinks that black artists and groups are "not allowed in the pop market" (although many blacks are million-sellers). "It's a pop market," she said right before the 21st Grammy Awards," and not many black people are allowed in the pop market. Look at the nominations this year—the Bee Gees and Olivia Newton-John."

Roberta Flack singles: "Will You Still Love Me Tomorrow?" (with Donny Hathaway), "You've Lost That Lovin' Feeling." On LP: *Take Three, Roberta Flack and Donny Hathaway*.

FLEETWOOD MAC

Not long ago at a recording studio in Los Angeles, The Village Recorder, the son of a friend of mine was putting together a syndicated radio show, *The History of Album Rock*. Studio costs there run $20,000 a week. The structure is not much to look at, but inside it's a palace of electronics; good-looking, comfortable furniture; and modern lighting. In another part of the building was Fleetwood Mac, a pop group that's made a lot of music history. It was busy at work on their long awaited two-LP album scheduled to appear after *Rumours*. *Rumours* was the monster smash on Warner Bros. Records.

Fleetwood Mac is your typical full-service rock band. They sing, they record, they play concerts, they write much of their own material. Once based in England, they now call California their home. It's members are: Christine McVie (keyboard, vocals); Lindsey Buckingham (guitar, vocals); Stevie Nicks (vocals); John McVie (bass); Mick Fleetwood (drums). Its biggest hit so far was the 1977 plati-

num album, *Rumours*, which has sold more than 12 million copies. *The Village Voice* called it "the most durable pop music ever put on plastic."

Mick (Michael) is the so-called "Mother Hen" of the group. He's the son of a former Royal Air Force wing commander. He was born in Cornwall, England, on June 24, 1947. But he's lived in a lot of places. He lived in Cairo for three years and later spent time in Norway, when his dad worked for NATO.

He went to boarding schools. As a teenager he fenced and played soccer (goalie). His father bought him drums and Mick fell in love with them. He left school at 15 and took off for London. There he built up a one-man decorating business. But he kept up with his music. He played drums with different groups.

There's a loose division of labor in the group. Mick Fleetwood and John McVie provide the strong rhythm section. Christine McVie is an effective singer and keyboard player. Stevie Nicks, the glamour girl of the group, and Lindsey stand out with what *The Hit Parader* calls "plaintive vocal duets and creamy harmonies." Sometimes the feminine voicings of Christine and Stevie are featured.

Fleetwood was formed in 1975. Its founding members were guitarist Peter Green, John McVie, and Mick Fleetwood. They were once in John Mayall's Bluesbreakers, based on the American blues. The first name of the new group was lumpy, Peter Green's Fleetwood Mac. Later on, Jeremy Spencer, a guitarist, signed on and so did another guitarist, Danny Kirwain. What they played years ago was the electric blues, their version of black blues, highly amplified.

However, in 1968 they became more contemporary, more rock. In 1968 they had one of their first hits, an instrumental. "The Albatross." This was followed by "Man of the World," "Oh, Well" (which got on the U.S. charts too), and "Green Manalishi."

As they rose higher and higher, so did personal problems. Peter Green left because of a spiritual crisis. Later on Jeremy Spencer disappeared while on a tour in the U.S. and joined a religious sect, The Children of God. There were more changes ahead until the present lineup. Pretty Stevie Nicks and Lindsey Buckingham were added to the group when Mick Fleetwood heard a tape of theirs in the U.S. So now, the British group is part American. With the addition of Nicks and Buckingham they got additional writer-singer strength.

Single record hits: "Don't Stop," "Gold Dust Woman," "Go Your Own Way," "Over My Head," "Say You Love Me." On LP: *Original (Fleetwood Mac 1967), Sire, Rumours,* and *Tusk.*

FOREIGNER

TWO YEARS AGO THERE WAS NO FOREIGNER.
TODAY, FOREIGNER HAS SOLD OVER
8 MILLION ALBUMS
—*Billboard* ad

Years ago, the word "foreigner" had bad vibrations. Today it's the name of a smash rock group. They released their first LP on March 8, 1977. Because it was a debut album, they called it simply *Foreigner*. Pop fans took to it. It sold a remarkable number of copies for an unknown band—more than three million on Atlantic Records.

Foreigner is a mix of six veteran British and U.S. musicians and singers. It got underway in 1976. Mick Jones began organizing the group whose members are: Mick Jones (from Britain, lead guitar, vocals, co-producer), Ian McDonald (from England, lead guitar, vocals, co-producer), Lou Gramm (U.S. lead vocals), Al Greenword (U.S., keyboard synthesizer), Ed Gagliardi, (U.S. bass, vocals) Dennis Elliot (from England, drums).

Just to show that it wasn't a fluke, the second LP of Foreigner hit the charts too. *Double Vision*,

brought out in 1978, has sold more than two million copies, so far. A single drawn from it, "Hot Blooded" reached the Top Ten. Not only that, they have also done well in personal appearances and at concerts.

Mick Jones: "We're far more interested in trying to make music that will send shivers down our own spines than in trying to be the Perfect Rock Group." Ian McDonald adds that the group tries to reach audiences rather than confuse them with avant garde gimmickry. The songs done by Foreigner, as he puts it, are "very accessible . . . rather than being spacey and intellectual. They are just very good songs. At face value, they are simple because they are easily grasped, but the more you hear them the more you hear how we worked on the arrangements."

Foreigner creates its own material. Speaking of *Double Vision*, Mick Jones says, "I happened to write a good deal of the songs. But a lot of them I wrote with Lou, and Lou and Ian wrote one together." Other members of the band also contributed, and continue to write.

In 1978 the group made an ambitious "Around the World in 42 Days Tour." They did shows and promotional shtick in Japan, Hong Kong, Greece, Germany, and England. It started off with a gig at California Jan. 11, where they performed for a huge crowd. The boys, who've been around, are pros who realize the necessity of touring and promotion to make sure Foreigner sells records.

Single hits by Foreigner include: "Feels Like the First Time," "Cold as Ice," and "Long Way From Home."

PETER FRAMPTON

I t was something you never see in a travel poster.
In the summer of '78, Peter Frampton was va-
cationing in the Bahamas. A car he was driving
on a rain-slick road spun out of control and
crashed, injuring his side and his right arm. The
guitar hand. He was flown to a New York hospital
and treated by specialists. Now recovered, this pop
idol has resumed his career, giving concerts and
making recordings.

Smallish in frame, Peter is esthetic-looking
with blondish, curly, long hair. He doesn't look
his age. Though British, he lives in the U.S. His
home is a sprawling 53-acre estate in Croton-on-
the-Hudson, slightly north of New York City. He
enjoys walking, watching TV, seeing movies, and
listening to records. He has an easygoing dispo-
sition, and is known as rock's "Mr. Nice Guy."

The singer-guitarist-songwriter was born April
22, 1950, in Beckenham, Kent, England. He started
playing guitar at the age of 8. At 14 he was already
playing in small British clubs (somehow managing

to escape the notice of the British legal authorities governing child labor). Teenagers, particularly the girls, liked his golden-haired looks. When he was with the Herd, a teenage rock band, he was known as "The Face."

In England, Frampton was associated with the Herd and later Humble Pie. Both groups created quite a stir and led to recordings that hit the British charts. His father helped negotiate his first contract. That was for 15 pounds a week, or roughly $50.

Close to his parents, Peter recently told *Co-Ed* magazine, "My father is an artist, my grandmother was a singer, and my brother, Clive, just got his degree in design. I went to England just to see him receive it. My mother is very musical too, so I have a lot of creativity behind me and my parents encouraged me."

Musically, Frampton is a mix, capable of both soft and hard rock. On stage, he is a strong performer, but he doesn't do the snarling pantherlike act of other rock performers.

In 1971 he cut his first solo album, *Wind of Change*. His second was *Frampton's Camel*. They didn't sell too well, and Peter was discouraged and low on money. He even thought he would forget trying to make it as a solo artist, and just become a studio musician. During those days he even pawned some of his possessions.

With a new U.S. manager, Dee Anthony, behind him, Frampton decided to take another crack at making it. He cut another album titled *Frampton*, released in 1975. It did very well, and then he followed it up with concerts throughout the U.S.

In 1976, with his fifth LP, *Frampton Comes Alive*, Peter became a superstar. The LP sold about 12 million copies. That year his records, concerts, and posters generated $67 million worth of revenue.

In 1978 he co-starred in his first film, *Sgt. Pepper's Lonely Hearts Club Band*. The critics rapped the picture, but the soundtrack of the film sold pretty well. In 1979 his long-time girlfriend, Penny McCall of Wisconsin, sued him for 50 percent of his millions. She claimed she helped him during a low point in his career ("lent him money"); then Peter "forgot our love."

Frampton on LP: *Frampton Comes Alive*, *I'm in You*.

ART GARFUNKEL

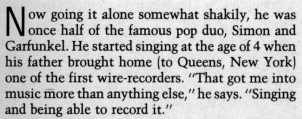

N ow going it alone somewhat shakily, he was once half of the famous pop duo, Simon and Garfunkel. He started singing at the age of 4 when his father brought home (to Queens, New York) one of the first wire-recorders. "That got me into music more than anything else," he says. "Singing and being able to record it."

Art was born in Newark, New Jersey, Nov. 5, 1941. His family later moved to Queens, NY, where he met Paul Simon in P.S. 163. The two of them started to hang out together and sing pop songs, first Everly Brothers songs, then rhythm and blues and rock. The two practiced in a basement, and then cut demos. Their first 45 was a modest hit, "Hey, School Girl" under the name of Tom and Jerry. No hits followed.

Fearful of the insecurity of the pop record, Art, tallish with upswept, light curly hair, went on to Columbia University. He majored in art history and architecture. It wasn't hard because Garfunkel likes the process of learning. In 1962 he teamed up once more with his neighborhood friend, Paul Simon. "Up until then we sang and wrote rock and roll songs together," he says, "but suddenly one of us could write poetic folk songs. I really connected with that. So the rejoining, after several years, was on the basis of the two of us as singers and Paul as the songwriter."

There followed a streak of non-rock single hits and gold records. These include such albums as *Wednesday Morning 3 A.M.*; *Sounds of Silence*; *Parsley, Sage, Rosemary and Thyme*; the soundtrack from *The Graduate*; *Bookends*; and *Bridge Over Troubled Water*. While not easily capsuled, these LPs reflected a soft vision of love, sorrow, people, and city life. In 1978, though officially split up, they traveled to England to receive the Britannia Award for the finest single piece of recorded music over the past 25 years (1952–1977). They won it for *Bridge Over Troubled Water*, a modern gospel-type song.

Of the past, Garfunkel says: "They were fabulous years. I'm proud of singing those great songs. . . . Paul did much of the talking and the guitar playing. I did the coloration, the harmonies."

Art is now married and working on his solo career. Since the break up of the team in 1970 he's cut several albums including *Angel Clare* ('73) and *Watermark* ('78). *Watermark* hit the charts. In '79 he released *Fate for Breakfast*. Garfunkel has also had roles in two films so far, *Catch 22* and *Carnal Knowledge*. Hyping himself, he ventured out on a solo tour not long ago and did well. Reviewing a concert he gave at Carnegie Hall *The New York*

Times wrote: "an original and compelling song stylist and an understated but remarkably musical vocal technician." You don't get screaming with Art, nor mashed lyrics. He considers himself "a baritone tenor."

On LP: *Angel Clare*, *Watermark*, *Fate for Breakfast*.

LEIF GARRETT

Most Jewish-Italian-Irish-Hispanic mothers would try to fatten him up. They'd feed him chicken soup, pasta, corned beef and cabbage, chick peas. But millions of young girls love Leif (pronounced "Lafe") just as he is. Thinnish, 5'9", about 130 pounds, with blue eyes and soft golden hair, he is basically an actor. But recently he's tried to become a pop star, where a lot of money is to be made. As he puts it in *Rock Stars,* "I want to be a rock singer."

Of modest musical talent, Leif carries a tune and clearly states the lyric. He plays guitar. With his popularity all his fans want is to have his photograph on the cover of an LP and hear his voice. His first single record was "Surfin' USA" followed by "Runaround Sue." He's cut two LPs, *Feel the Need* and *Leif Garrett.* In 1979 he had a single hit on Scotti Records, "I Was Made for Dancin'."

Leif was born Nov. 8, 1961. His mother's name is Carolyn. He has a sister, Dawn Lynn. He first

came to public attention as an actor on TV with appearances on *The Odd Couple*, *Three for the Road*, and *Family*. He was also seen in the movie comedy, *Bob and Carol and Ted and Alice*.

Along with Shaun Cassidy and Andy Gibb, Leif is part real, part media-creation, part skillful publicity. His picture is carried in hundreds of thousands of those see-through plastic pages in girls' wallets. The printing presses roll, turning out posters of him. Color pinup portraits of him appear as centerfolds in teen magazines, and can be seen on the walls of many bedrooms and "rec rooms" where young girls are in residence. In his case, the hype machine and the teen media have collaborated in building him up to teen-idol status.

For the past few years fan magazines have run such features as "Leif Garrett's Personal Photo Album," "Leif Garrett's Fan Club," and a book called *The Secrets of Leif Garrett*. Leif is being packaged like breakfast cereal, but if he minds it, he doesn't publicly complain. He can be contacted by writing: Leif Garett, J. Carter Gibson Agency, 9000 Sunset Blvd., Los Angeles, CA 90069.

Early in 1978 he went on a European tour to expand his audience base in relation to records. There he did interviews, TV, visited deejays, autographed records in Luxembourg, answered questions in fan magazines, and sang on German TV. Later he was set to go on a U.S. concert tour but he got pneumonia. Pop music is strongly on his mind. Often he wears a sports jacket with the logo of Atlantic (ATCO) Records on the back. A normal day for Leif is packed with meetings, rehearsals, interviews, photo sessions, talking with his agents. He dates many Hollywood lovelies, including Tatum O'Neal.

Of course, his fans are crazy about him. Letters to the editor rave about him. One glowing sample from a girl in Brooklyn, N.Y.: "He sings great. He acts great. He talks great. He walks great. He dresses great. Face it folks—he is great!"

Leif enjoys soccer, horseback riding, Led Zeppelin, *M☆A☆S☆H*, reruns of *Lucy*, and backgammon.

Sample LPs: *Feel the Need* (Scotti), *Leif Garett* (Atlantic).

CRYSTAL GAYLE

In pop music, happiness is a recording contract. And bliss is when a recording personality actually wins an award. That's happening increasingly to lovely brunette Crystal Gayle. On January 12, 1979, she was honored (along with the Bee Gees and Linda Ronstadt) as favorite female country vocalist at the 6th Annual American Music Awards.

Like many of today's pop artists, she's a crossover artist, mixing pop, country, and the blues. Probably her biggest hit so far has been the single "Don't Make My Brown Eyes Blue." It sold more than 1½ million copies and reached number one on both the country and pop charts. She recently starred in her own TV special.

5'3" and in her mid-20's, Ms. Gayle was born in the small town of Painstville, Kentucky. As a child, she was surrounded by music since all of her four brothers and three sisters were, as a UA biography puts it, "involved in music." Her sister is country superstar Loretta Lynn. At 4, her family moved to Wabash, Indiana. During her high school years she performed in church and sang at civic functions. After graduation, Crystal signed her first recording contract with Decca Records, now MCA. Her first single, "I've Cried (The Blue Right Out of My Eyes)," hit the Top 20 of the country charts. When it was re-released in 1977 it raced up the country charts again.

In January 1973, Crystal moved over to United Artists Records. Her first UA single, "Restless," received heavy airplay and was a country chart item. That gave her entry to the personal appearance market. Crystal found herself performing in many of the top nightclubs across the country. In 1978 both the Academy of Country Music and the Country Music Association named her "Outstanding Female Vocalist."

She's got a nice sense of delivery and a clean, clear voice. Her physical beauty adds to her appeal and could make her a movie star. The singer-songwriter is married. With her husband, Bill (who is studying law), she lives in Nashville. Although she is quite a homemaker, most of her spare time is spent writing songs and trying out new musical ideas.

Crystal has been seen on practically every big-league TV show except perhaps the seven o'clock news. It's helped her win pop music fans as well as Nashville-oriented record-buyers. She's appeared on *The Tonight Show*, *Merv Griffin*, *Mike Douglas*, and *Dinah* shows. She's also been booked on many TV specials, including *The Dean Martin Christmas Special*, *The Wayne Newton Special*, *The Osmond Brothers Special*, *The Lou Rawls*

Special, and *The 25th Anniversary of the Wonderful World of Disney.* She has also hosted *Midnight Special* and an NBC Special, *Country Night of Stars.*

On LP: *Crystal Gayle, Somebody Loves You, Crystal* (including "One More Time," "Do It All Over Again," "Never Miss a Good Thing"), *We Must Believe in Magic* (a 1978 platinum-seller that contained the hit single, "Don't Make My Brown Eyes Blue"), *When I Dream.*

GLORIA GAYNOR

The gimmick was simple. The artist: Gloria Gaynor. The company: Polydor. The year: 1975. The LP: *Never Can Say Goodbye.* The lyrics were typical pop-love stuff set to a disco beat. The gimmick was to release the LP without the little bands that separate one tune from another.

"For the first time," according to Polydor, "an album had been programmed for nonstop dancing with one song running smoothly into the next without a pause." Disco deejays spun an entire side of Gloria's pulsating LP night after night. It became a million-seller and helped spark the dance craze in the U.S. and around the world.

Of course, the continuous music gimmick wasn't the only thing that put it over. There were the arrangements, and Gloria's rich, strong voice. The 5'6½" disco star was born Sept. 7, 1946, in Newark, New Jersey, where she was raised. She's one of seven children (five brothers and a sister). Her father sang briefly in vaudeville. At 8 she thought of being a singer.

At 13 she "studied" with recordings, because she couldn't afford singing lessons. "I loved Nat Cole, Sarah Vaughn, and Marvin Gaye. It always amazed me how they could sing a thousand words in a line and you could understand every one."

At 18 Gloria received her first offer to sing professionally. A group that had just lost their singer wanted her to fill the post. The gig was in Canada. "I'd never even been out of Newark, but I quit my job as an accountant and told everybody I was going to be a big star. We were there two weeks. Then I worked one week in New Jersey and that was it for my career for almost three years."

One night Gloria visited a club in Newark with a neighbor. The band was playing a song Gloria knew, and the neighbor, without telling Gloria, convinced them to call her to the stage. They were so impressed that they hired Gloria that night. She traveled with that band throughout the Midwest, then formed a group of her own, City Life. They played the East Coast circuit, working nightclubs, supper clubs and hotels, playing six shows a night, six nights a week. In two years, she had just two weeks off.

Gloria was signed by Columbia Records and in 1974 recorded the single "Honey Bee." Later she switched to MGM/Polydor Records.

She believes that as time goes by disco will have something to say other than "let's dance" or "let's get together." Her hits include "Never Can Say Goodbye," "Reach Out I'll Be There," "Casanova Brown," and "I Will Survive." Gloria has toured a great deal and is especially popular in Italy,

Spain, France, Germany, Belgium, and England, as well as Mexico, South America, New Zealand, and Australia. In the spring and early summer of '79 she went on a 50-city U.S. tour with the Village People, the Jacksons, and Lou Rawls.

Gloria likes to write lyrics. She wrote the words to "Love Affair" in her LP, *Park Avenue Sounds*. Other LPs: *Experience Gloria Gaynor*, *I Got You*, *Glorious*, *Love Tracks*.

★

ANDY GIBB

★

"I owe my interest in music to my brothers," says RSO Records star, Andy Gibb. One of today's top teen idols, he is a member of the first family of pop, the Bee Gees, which include his brothers (Maurice, Barry, and Robin). Born Mar. 5, 1959, in Manchester, England, he now lives in Miami. His hair is light brown. He has an easy, winning smile. His eyes are brown with golden flecks.

His first U.S. record was a hit, "I Just Want to Be Your Everything," and so was his first LP, *Flowing Rivers*. His first movie was *Sgt. Pepper's Lonely Hearts Club Band*. Like his brothers, Andy accents melodic tunes with a rocking beat. In personal appearances he dances, and his simple footwork turns his fans (mostly girls) on.

What kind of music does he like? He has told *Teen-Machine*'s fan book, "I really enjoy melody and good lyrics. Old-fashioned ballads are wonderful and will always be around."

His mother was a singer; his father was a drummer and leader of a big band. When he was six months old, his family moved to Australia. In 1967, at age nine, Andy and his family moved back to England, where he went to school. In 1970 the restless Gibb clan, who love the water, took up residence on Ibiza, an island off the coast of Spain where Andy started performing at a local tourist bar. In 1973 Andy formed a rock 'n' roll band on The Isle of Man (off England). They played for a year in the island's two major nightclubs. Later he sang and recorded in Australia. His first Australian single was "Words and Music." Still later, Robert Stigwood, RSO president, signed him up.

Andy plays drums. He sings in an intimate voice of limited range; he's no belter. Mostly he records in Miami's Criteria Studios. His brothers guide his musical career, providing him with arranging suggestions and songs. His brother, Barry, wrote the first hit that launched Andy's career, "I Just Want to Be Your Everything." He is poised and confident on stage. But when he finished a personal appearance, he often asks if he sounded okay. He wants to do a good job. Rock critics think he's a so-so singer.

Andy is a true "teen idol." This is not a putdown but means simply that he is exceptionally popular among 12 to 17 year olds. Fan magazines follow him around as Sherlock Holmes pursued the evil Dr. Moriarty. Every detail about him is covered and analyzed under such captions as "He's A Good Friend," "He's Sensitive," "He's A Fitness Freak," "He's Very Romantic," "He's A Family Man," "He's Easily Hurt," "He Takes Risks" (16 magazine).

Andy has a daughter, Peta. He is divorced from his wife, Kim, whom he married in 1976 at the age of 18. He is partial to tank tops and shiny athletic jackets. He is fond of American-type food and drink—hamburgers, shakes, and fries. If there's a concert around, he likes to take it in. He also enjoys quiet evenings watching TV. Along with recording and concerts, Andy has guested on many TV shows. He has a winning smile. Miami, known for its senior citizens, is especially happy that Andy (and the Bee Gees) have chosen to put down roots there. For it gives that Florida city a youth connection.

Andy on LP: *Flowing Rivers, Shadow Dancing.*

★

THE GRATEFUL DEAD

★

The Grateful Dead is a West Coast legend with a cult following. *Variety* has described it as a rock band that's still fiercely anti-commercial with "laid-back country-tinged melodies." A flashy-type group, they do a lot of their numbers deadpan.

It's a vocal and instrumental band that put San Francisco on the pop music map, along with Jefferson Airplane (now Jefferson Starship). The group formed in an odd way. In 1964 Garcia, then a folk musician, got together a folk band, Mother McGreen's Uptown Jug Champions. It wasn't too successful. Then a Palo Alto, California, music merchant offered them electronic instruments on the condition they switch to amplified rock. Musicians were added to the group, and soon Garcia was into the rock scene, into sonic booms. They also were heavily into drugs, and they later did weird, moody numbers that came to be known as "psychedelic rock." For a while, they even ran their own rock auditorium, the Carousel Ballroom in San Francisco.

The top man is heavily bearded singer-guitarist, Jerry (Jerome) Garcia. "I'm 36 now," he told rock reporter, Lou Neil Jr. of the *New York Post*, "but I've been playing the guitar since I was 15. I really didn't get serious about it until '63 and '64. It was then we started playing around the Bay Area. Back then we were known as the Warlocks, not the Dead. That was before we became the Grateful Dead. We were simply a bar band on the Coast."

At first they recorded for Warner Bros. Later they released under their own label. Now they're with Arista. Oddly enough, and this happens with a lot of rock bands, they are more popular live— in concert—than they are on records. The band mixes country, blues, and rock. On stage they seem to spark an audience into getting up and turning an auditorium into a disco. Not long ago, for example, they played Madison Square Garden in New York City. In the course of the concert, they played the funky "Shakedown Street" from a new LP, *Eyes of the World*. Soon the entire audience was on its feet and dancing.

This California-based band is famed for its long marathon concerts. Some of them last four hours. As one observer put it, sometimes one of their concerts is an endurance contest for band—and audience.

Its discography includes such singles as: "Me and My Uncle," "Everybody's Doing That Rag," "King Bee," "Good Lovin'." Sample LPs: *History of the Grateful Dead*, *Jerry Garcia* (solo LP), *Best of Grateful Dead*, *Shakedown Street*.

AL GREEN

From Arkansas, singer-songwriter born in 1946, Al Green is in the pop soul tradition. He records on a label with one of the most informal names, Hi. At the age of 8 he heard a Sam Cooke record on the radio. That inspired him to become a singer. At 9 he was a member of a homemade family gospel group with his brothers. Later, his family moved to Grand Rapids, Michigan. There, while in high school, he organized his own pop group. Later he put together a musical combo called Al Green and the Creations, which worked small black clubs and black fraternal organizations in the South and Midwest.

His first single was "Back Up Train" in 1967, on Hot Line, a small independent label. The record managed to hang in there and finally hit the soul charts in 1969. His big breakthrough song was something he wrote himself, "Tired of Being Alone." It zoomed up to number one nationally, and got him a gold record.

Since then the handsome, boyish Al Green has

become "a name." On stage he is quite something to watch. *Billboard* gave this picture of an Al Green appearance in the Dorothy Chandler Pavilion in Los Angeles, Lincoln Center West:

"On the eve of Valentine's Day, Green shook the chandeliers of the sold out Pavilion with a high-energy show that helped his audience forget the long delay. Before he began to sing he was presented with official proclamations of Al Green Day. His hit, "Love," was the opening of what proved to be a grand demonstration of his vocal control and stage movements. His 10-song presentation never faltered for even a moment and each song was an unrestrained outporing of energy."

Like many pop show people Green is fond of flashy clothes. At that Los Angeles concert, for example, he wore a shimmering, silver satin outfit. He is also known for "cute" show-biz shtick. One of his bits is throwing out red roses to women admirers after a set.

Some consider him one of the half-dozen prime geniuses of soul music. Robert Christgrau, of *Newsday*, once wrote, "His genius is in his rhythms. . . . He's best in personal performance. The overall effect is an artist whose intelligence and humor are well integrated into his records, and they only become clear in person."

His singing style varies from gospel and rhythm and blues to country to straightaway pop. He is famed for his high moans.

His home base in the seventies has been Memphis, Georgia. He tours music tents, arenas, and theaters, including Harlem's Apollo. His songs mostly deal with love, love, love. While that's a big area of human interest, it is also very narrow.

His LPs include: *I'm Still in Love with You, Call Me, Greatest Hits, Can't Get Next to You, Full of Fire.* His hit singles: "Here I Am (Come and Take Me)," "Let's Stay Together."

MERLE HAGGARD

Labor songs, songs about working people, finding a job, low pay, are a part of folk music, soul, musical comedy, rock, and country music. There are many work songs with a blues beat. Not long ago there was a musical on Broadway called *Working*. And recently country singer Johnny Paycheck depicted an unhappy worker in his hit, "Take This Job and Shove It." Similarly, Merle Haggard has produced an LP sympathetic to the ordinary guy (and gal), *A Workingman Can't Get Nowhere Today*.

Merle Haggard, an earthy country singer-guitarist, was born in Bakersfield, California, on April 6, 1937. "When I was a child," he remembers, "we used to sit around the radio on Saturday nights and listen to Grand Ole Opry."

At 14, he ran away from home to see the world. For eight years he wandered through the West and the Southwest, working in oil fields, driving a truck, getting on and off freight trains, picking cotton, and getting into trouble.

"I was a pretty wild kid," he says. "I love excitement, I even did some time," he once told *The Los Angeles Times*. "I'm not proud of what I did. I wouldn't recommend it to anyone else, but I do believe I benefited from my experiences."

In the 1960s he got started in his hometown, singing and playing guitar in Bakersfield in little clubs patronized by folks who came up North from the South and Southwest. In 1963 he recorded for a small label, Tally Records. His first release sold about 200 records, but the next one, "Sing Me a Sad Song," made the country music charts.

Eventually he signed up with Capitol. His rough, leathery voice is one of the most famous among country music fans. Many of the topics of his songs are from things he's felt and experienced. There's "Mama Tried" (about his wild teen days), "Branded Man" (the way people look at those who've served time), and poverty ("Hungry Eyes").

A lot of Haggard's songs go back to the depression of the thirties. But they are still appropriate. "There's no depression, but people still have hard times," he says.

One of his smash hits was an anti-hippie ballad that was a number-one song, "Okie from Muskogee." He lives out on the West Coast in a home not far from the Kern River. He loves to fish. He's married to singer Bonnie Owens, with whom he recorded *Just Between the Two of Us*.

Among his LPs: *Mama Tried, Strangers, Sing Me Back Home, Branded Man, I'm a Lonesome Fugitive, The Best of Merle Haggard, I'm Always on a Mountain, Pride in What I Am, The Way It Was, Songs I'll Always Sing*.

MARVIN HAMLISCH

★

As a young boy growing up in Manhattan, Marvin showed raw musical talent. The Hamlisches had a family friend, a pop songwriter, Freddie Spielman. One night Spielman was having dinner with the family and Hamlisch's mother asked Freddie to take young Marvin and introduce him to Tin Pan Alley music publishers. Freddie was embarrassed and not certain whether he should take such a young boy to make the rounds of his contacts; so he didn't. As the years went by, Marvin broke through as a hit song composer. The mother never let Spielman forget it. She would say, "Freddie, Marvin made it without you."

Composer-pianist Marvin Hamlisch is atop the pop world: winner of two Oscars, four Grammys, nine Tonys (the Broadway award), and a Pulitzer Prize. It wasn't all easy. On the way up, publishers showed him the door and one of his biggest hits almost never got done. He wrote the title song of the movie, *The Way We Were* starring Barbra Streisand. "It was one of Barbra's biggest hits," he says [it sold more than 2 million], "but I had to beg Barbra to do it. She never wanted to do it."

From his piano have come single hits, TV specials, two big Broadway shows, and 18 movie scores (so far). For films, he's scored everything from Woody Allen comedies to James Bond thrillers *(The Spy Who Loved Me)* out of which came the hit, "Nobody Does It Better." Perhaps his best large work has been the score of the Pulitzer Prize-winning Broadway musical, *A Chorus Line*. Successful all over the world, it will soon be a movie. Songs of his have been recorded by Kenny Rogers, Carly Simon, and Liza Minnelli.

Recently, this friendly, humorous man who also performs on TV *(Merv Griffin, Mike Douglas,* music tents, "pops" concerts, on records) added to his laurels. He wrote the music for still another Broadway hit musical, *They're Playing Our Song.* Neil Simon wrote the "book" (story line and dialogue). And it's based loosely on Marvin's real-life relationship with a young, brunette lyricist, Carole Bayer Sager. In the show, Robert Klein plays Hamlisch, and Lucie Arnaz (Lucille Ball's daughter) plays Carole Bayer Sager. (Miss Sager also wrote the lyrics for the show.)

Born in New York City in 1945, his father played the accordian at Viennese parties. Marvin entered Juilliard (a New York music conservatory) at age seven, and stayed there 11 years. Later he went on to Queens College to study theory and modern music. While going to school, Marvin was already playing "gigs" and acting as rehearsal pianist. At 16 he wrote his first pop fit for Leslie Gore, "Sunshine, Lollipops, and Rainbows."

He can compose in practically every style—sophisticated, pop, soft rock, heavy rock. However, he is a deep believer in melody, and thinks that the melody writer can make it in today's pop music scene if he/she writes good tunes and then puts them in a contemporary context, even using rock. About melody he says, "I believe in making people cry, in strong melody." He adds, "You see I really want to write standards, not just the hit of the moment."

His single hits include: "The Way We Were," "California Nights," "Nobody Does It Better." On LP. *A Chorus Line* (cast album), *The Sting* (adapted from music by Scott Joplin) and *They're Playing Our Song* (cast album).

MICHAEL
JACKSON

He used to be the cute little kid that sang and danced with his brothers, the Jackson Five. Today, he's all grown up, a record personality on his own, as well as a movie actor. His big screen break came when he appeared in *The Wiz*. He played The Scarecrow. Recently, he landed the lead role as the late Bill Robinson, the famous black dancer, a star in vaudeville who also acted in films with Shirley Temple. Michael also got a big part in the upcoming movie version of the famous Broadway hit musical, *A Chorus Line*.

The most successful of all the Jackson family, Michael was born Aug. 29, 1958. He still performs with the Jacksons and is their lead singer. He is the darling of the fan magazines and has been linked romantically with many young female personalities. On stage he resembles a kind of young

Sammy Davis, Jr. He sings, he dances, he mugs. Besides recording with his family, he's also made many records as a solo artist. One of his early hits as a solo performer was "Got to Be There."

He enjoys photography, sports, and girls. Along with his brothers, Jackie, Tito, Jermaine, and Marlon, he was born in Gary, Indiana. Actually, there were nine children. His father, Joe Jackson, a crane operator, liked music and in his spare time wrote songs and played the guitar. Their mother, Katherine, liked to sing the blues and country and western tunes.

They lived in a poor neighborhood. As the kids grew up, they started to sing and became one of Gary's better amateur pop groups. One day in 1969 the black mayor of Gary told Diana Ross about the group. She told Berry Gordy, Jr., about them, and before long, Motown signed them up. Records followed, also TV shows, such as Ed Sullivan, and right up there was Michael, singing and dancing. Their first hit single was "I Want You Back."

During the early years, it was young Michael who got the most attention. As Motown once said, "While all the boys contribute equally to the act, it is Michael who creates the most stir, both because of his tender age and the excitement he generates on stage."

In 1971 young Michael turned solo artist as well. Today, Michael and his family live in California. Several of his brothers are married. Most of them still perform as a pop group, but they have broken away from Motown and now record for Columbia. So does Michael. He and his brothers have starred in an animated cartoon TV series which is still in reruns.

His singles include "Ben," (movie title song). On LP: *Got to Be There, The Wiz* (original soundtrack).

JEFFERSON STARSHIP

Where are the pop groups of yesteryear? Where are the Byrds, the Association, the Rascals, Paul Revere and the Raiders, the Kingston Trio, the Monkees? Many members of these groups are out of the business. John Lennon of the Beatles is raising cattle in the East. Some hug their scrap-books as if they were a security blanket. Jefferson Airplane have spawned a sub-group—Jefferson Starship.

The old/new group still operates out of San Fran-cisco. It functions with a lot of new musicians. The big names of the past—Marty Balin (painter, singer), Grace Slick, Jorma Kaukonen, Paul Kant-ner, Jack Casady, and Spencer Dryden—are almost faint memories. Sometimes singer Grace Slick joins the new group. Sometimes Paul Kantner will come in from his big estate to audit rehearsals.

But it's not what it used to be.

In the 1960s, Jefferson Airplane was the powerful voice of the California counter-culture. The lyrics they sang were often unusual in form and content. And they were also anti-establishment. In many ways, the Airplane was the typical rock band of the angry decade. It was into protest, drugs, into a communal-type of operation with headquarters in a Victorian mansion. Its sound, as RCA put it, was "drawn from jazz, folk, Indian ragas, Bach, and blue-grass." Its lyrics were often super-serious, political, and literary. In one song, "Volunteers of America," it called for a radical re-shaping of U.S. institutions.

However, eventually the wings and wheels came off the Jefferson Airplane. People left to do solo albums, and to form other groups (Hot Tuna). There were other projects too. In the 1970s Grace Slick and Paul Kantner reunited to form Jefferson Starship, which records on Grunt Records and is distributed by RCA.

The new group started in the fall of 1974 with the release of its first LP, *Dragonfly.* In 1975 Marty Balin came back into the group. The release that followed was *Red Octopus.* It was a monster hit and sold more than 2½ million copies—a number-one album. It's a group that takes its time. One of its releases, titled *Earth,* took one year to complete.

To reach a new generation of record-buyers and concert-goers, the Jefferson goes on tour. Not long ago, they gave a concert at the Nassau Coliseum, Uniondale, L.I., N.Y. It went off pretty well. *Variety* wrote: "The Jefferson Starship ran through a full program of old and new material in crowd-pleasing form."

The current lineup (subject to change) is Slick (the lead vocalist), Kantner and Balin (the golden oldies), along with newcomers Craig Chaquico, David Friedberg (keyboard, bass guitar), John Barbetta (drummer), Pete Serars (bass guitar), and Jesse Barris. In concert, and for other projects, Jefferson Starship sometimes uses two horns.

Those who want to catch up with the old days can read *Jefferson Airplane*, by Ralph Gleason. To check out the new unit, there are the new albums: *Jefferson Starship, Gold, Earth*.

WAYLON
JENNINGS

Disc jockeys talk a lot but they seldom can carry a tune. One exception is Waylon Jennings, a superstar who used to spin discs in the Southwest. Now an RCA recording artist, he is a rugged, rebellious, outspoken Texan. It's taken him quite a while to achieve across-the-board public acceptance. Now he's got it. He mixes country and rock, and performs it in a rough and dark-voiced style. Musically, he digs Bob Dylan, the Beatles, Joni Mitchell, and Chuck Berry, as well as country sounds.

The bearded singer-guitarist was born in Littlefield, Texas, June 15, 1937. As a kid, Waylon learned how to pick out tunes on a guitar. At 12, he was spinning platters on a Littlefield radio station as a disc jockey. During those years Waylon also sang and made personal appearances in that part of Texas, concentrating mostly on pop songs.

He didn't get into country music till he was about 17.

Later on he moved to a bigger city, Lubbock, Texas, a college town (Texas Tech), as disc jockey. There he met Buddy Holly, a country boy turned rock star. Buddy asked him to join his band as an electric bass player.

Waylon told *Blast,* a pop paper: "I was Buddy's protégé." However, he's somewhat critical of some of the Buddy Holly songs. "The lyrics are dated, really kind of bubble-gum. It was teenage stuff and Buddy himself laughed at some of the songs people are now taking seriously."

Waylon was in the band at the time 21-year-old Buddy died in a plane crash in 1959. In the 1960s Waylon formed his own group, "Waylon Jennings and The Waylors." RCA heard of him and his band, then based in Phoenix, Arizona, and signed him up. Waylon made RCA happy when he cut some hits right away: "That's the Chance I'll Have to Take," "Stop the World I Want to Get Off," and "Anita, You're Dreaming."

He continued making records, guesting on TV the next few years. He even made a movie, *Nashville Rebel.* Then RCA released his album, *The Outlaws,* and his fame expanded. The LP featured Waylon, his pal Willie Nelson, and Jessie Colter (Waylon's wife). By December of that year, it became the first album to come out of Nashville to be a platinum record; that is, it sold more than one million units (records, tapes, cassettes). A gold record is one that sells a million dollars worth of records, which could only be 300,000 units, depending on the retail price.

Circus, reviewing Waylon's *Sweet Memories,* wrote: "He isn't your standard tear-jerking country and western singer; if anything, his bittersweet songs have more sophistication in them than most of the usual Nashville range-riders."

Kris Kristofferson calls him "the best country singer in the world." *Seventeen* magazine says he is "The Humphrey Bogart of country music." A Los Angeles music critic says: "Waylon Jennings is one of the most exciting and distinctive country talents in years." Among Waylon's LP hits are: *Dreaming My Dreams, Are You Ready for the Country,* and *Ol' Waylon.*

BILLY JOEL

"In junior high," Billy Joel says, "you could be a collegiate, a hitter, or a brownie—the kid who wears brown shoes with white socks, carries a schoolbag, and always gets monitor jobs." A street kid on the tough side, Billy didn't turn out too badly. He turned his brawling instincts into music. Now he's a star singer-performer-pianist, a Columbia artist and talented author of one of the best contemporary songs around, "Just the Way You Are" (a Grammy Award-winner as "Song of the Year").

Born on May 9, 1949, William Martin Joel's parents were workingclass people in the post-war Long Island (New York) suburban settlement of Hicksville. When they saw his fascination with a Mozart piece at the tender age of 4 they enrolled him with a piano teacher. His father, a German-born engineer for the General Electric Company, loved the classics. Billy would test his father's tolerance for boggie woogie and stride piano, early indications of his feisty nature.

155

The classical piano lessons continued for a dozen years, stopping about the same time that Billy enlisted in his first rock 'n' roll band, the Echoes. In 1964 the Beatles' *A Hard Day's Night* brought the aspiring rocker's ambitions into focus. Socially, it was another story. "We were hitters, I mean I had a gang and that's what we did. They called us punks—we didn't call ourselves punks, we thought we were hoods."

Despite the rough atmosphere, Billy managed to stick to his music. He played gigs until the wee hours and showed up in class sleepy and unprepared. Since his father had left home when Billy was 7, his mother worked at day jobs through the years. To help out, Billy worked as a keyboard musician from his teen years on. He had some nonmusic jobs too, as a house painter, factory worker, even rock critic.

Joel missed the tenth anniversary of his high school reunion (class of '67). That night he performed on NBC's *Saturday Night Live*. He mentioned the high school reunion on TV. It's a constant theme with Joel. In the *Billy Joel Songbook* there are many references to the adolescent years, the diner hangouts, meeting old girlfriends.

His wife, Elizabeth, managed him. Billy signed up with Columbia in 1973. One of his first singles was "Piano Man," his impressions of working in a piano bar. Later, an LP with the same title became a gold record. In 1974 *Cash Box* chose him as "Best New Male Vocalist." In 1978 he cut another best-selling hit LP, *The Stranger*, a platinum record (one million copies sold).

His lyrics are impressionistic and storylike,

such as "Scenes from an Italian Restaurant." He's not addicted to rhymes; often the lyrics are sort of ad lib, free. Not all of his songs are autobiographical. He picks up material from people around him.

His heroes are Dave Brubeck, Oscar Peterson, and Ray Charles, all jazz artists. Though he counts himself one of "the street people," on stage he wears a tie and jacket. He kids rock performers who wear crazy clothes and use drugs. While he can be a rocker, his heart is in melody rather than dense loud sounds, amplified to frantic levels. "I'm a big melody freak," he says.

In March '79 he was part of a U.S. all-star combo of American pop stars and groups that performed in Havana, Cuba, at the Karl Marx Stadium. He was such a smash that a *People* magazine cover spotlighted him in its report on the Cuban Woodstock.

Billy Joel on LP: *Just the Way You Are, The Stranger, 52nd Street.*

ELTON JOHN

On Nov. 7, 1978, Elton John, superstar millionaire, was rushed by ambulance to a hospital after collapsing with severe chest pains while at home at Berkshire, west of London. An examination showed that Elton hadn't had a heart attack but was suffering from exhaustion and overwork. Some months later, Elton returned to performing and making records, but at a slower pace.

Captain Fantastic, as he is sometimes known, is a powerful performer. He pounds the piano. His singing is a mix of roaring, cooing, crooning. He has a strong baritone. On stage, he's entertained his fans with stage spectacle as well as rock. Once he showed up costumed as the Statue of Liberty holding a torch. Another time he did a concert on a stage set built to resemble a giant pulsating jukebox. Wearing crazy glasses, he played a silver fiberglas piano that changed colors.

Rock critics have been super-critical of Elton. They've called him a "music machine," "a Potatohead" *(Creem)*. *The New York Times* once ran a piece on him headed, "Bad Taste Is Good Business for Elton." But Elton has continued to go his own flamboyant way. Balding, he has had a painful hair transplant. A health freak, he is also co-owner of one of England's best soccer teams, the Watford Football Club. He records for MCA Records. In 1977 his earnings were reportedly $14 million.

The British singer-songwriter-pianist was born in Middlesex, England, Mar. 25, 1947. His real name is Reginald Kenneth Dwight. His father was an RAF squadron leader. His mother, Sheila, was a buyer of show music albums, the LPs of Frank Sinatra. As a youngster he took piano lessons. He was also fascinated by pop that he heard coming over British radio—rock, blues, country artists. Later on, he took up the organ and started playing with pickup rock bands. Much of the time he copied the styles of rock stars he heard. Later on, he started formal studies at the Royal Academy of Music.

In 1966 he hooked up with a group called Bluesology, led by John Baldry. Reg stayed with the group for about two years. By the late '60s he started to do bits that resembled country star Jerry Lee Lewis: he wore crazy clothes and banged the piano.

By 1969 he was getting himself noticed and he got a recording contract. Also, he collaborated on writing songs with lyricist Bernie Taupin. Elton John's first album was *Empty Sky* in 1969. His first U.S. tour was in 1970.

In '79 Elton returned to the recording scene with a new LP, *A Single Man*. On the LP he played electric keyboard (for the first time) and acted as co-producer. The record was a kind of "first" for Elton. It was the first time he didn't write with his famed lyricist Bernie Taupin. His collaborator was Gary Osborne. Singing backup vocals were members of his Watford soccer team.

At one point, Elton wore a button, "Back By Popular Demand." This was to stress that his return to performing was to please his fans. However, he's a changed Elton. He seems to have kissed good-bye the big-league tours with backup band, the complex travel schedules, the road managers, and the big hype machine. He told *Hit Parader:* "I do like doing the occasional show, must with piano. I guess I'm just a cynic about gigs these days. I feel that I've seen it all." He also reported that he's cutting out the crazy glasses; he's going to wear contact lenses.

Elton on LP: *Goodbye Yellow Brick Road, Greatest Hits, Vol. 1, Greatest Hits, Vol. 3, Honky Chateau, Elton John Tumbleweed Connection, Madman Across the Water, Friends* (movie soundtrack), *Don't Shoot Me, I'm Only the Piano Player.*

CAROLE KING

They call California the sun-kissed Tin Pan Alley. That's because so many record companies, groups, record producers, record studios, and music publishers are based there. It's also where many ex-New Yorkers now live and work. One of them is petite, Carole King. She was born in Brooklyn, Feb. 9, 1942. Carole (5'5") is one of pop's triple-threats. She writes words and music, she sings, and she plays piano.

While in high school, she picked up on the new pop coming in—the rhythm and blues singers, the records of Bill Haley, Fats Domino. Later she attended Queens College (N.Y.) where she was pretty good at math. Later, afternoons, she subwayed to Manhattan to try to break into the music business.

While making the rounds of publishers' offices, the Turf restaurant, she met Gerry Goffin, a lyricist. The young songwriters collaborated on a bunch of songs that became hits now considered golden oldies of the '60s: "Up on the Roof," "Locomotion," "Natural Woman." Their music and lyrics followed a grittier, almost black approach, even though Carole and Gerry were white. Among the artists that recorded Goffin-King songs were black artists and groups (The Drifters, Maxine Brown, The Chiffons) and white groups and personalities (Bobby Vee, Dusty Springfield).

It was a hectic, learning experience for Carole and Gerry. They wrote a lot of songs quickly to order. The publisher they worked for (Don Kirschner, presently a TV rock host-producer) found out who needed material, and he got Carol and Gerry to write songs to fit the image and approach of the particular performer or group. There were other songwriters writing to order too: Neil Diamond, Neil Sedaka, Howard Greenfield.

Under these pressured conditions, Carole sharpened her writing talents. Gerry, her collaborator, proposed, and the songwriters got married. They moved to New Jersey and had two children, both girls. While married they wrote a song for their baby-sitter, Eva, who had a group, The Cookies, called "Locomotion." It became a hit. In the early '60s Carole turned performer and cut her own album on a new label, Dimension. But at this point, the songwriting was more important.

In the mid-'60s, Carole and Gerry were divorced. Carole moved to the West Coast to start life anew and to raise her two daughters. (One of them, Louise, now writes songs and sings.) Carole went on as a solo writer (both music and words) and recording artist. In 1968 she cut her second album with a new group called The City, released by Ode Records. It didn't do too well. Then James Taylor suggested that she really go solo, without being part of a group, just play piano and sing her own songs. She okayed the idea and had several test engagements that went very well. This led to her solo album, *Carole King—Writer*.

In 1971 she put out *Tapestry*, a Grammy Award-winner and a multi-million seller. Now a Capitol Records artist, she continues to perform, record, and write. Two years ago she wrote a perky, successful score for the TV musical based on Maurice Sendak's marvelous book, *Really Rosie*. Among her most popular songs are: "You've Got a Friend" and "I Feel the Earth Move," both of which have been recorded by many artists and groups.

Carole on LP: *Rhymes and Reason, Music, Tapesty, Fantasy, Sample, Welcome.*

★

KISS

★

In February 1979, the youth division of the Gallup Poll released a study of 1,100 teenagers between 13 and 18 to discover who was their favorite rock group. According to this sample America's number-one favorite group was Kiss. The wild group who spend a fortune on make-up, props, costumes, and lighting beat out the Bee Gees and The Rolling Stones.

With such a romantic name, you'd expect soft lights, quiet music, and flowers. But with Kiss you get faces painted white with devil's heads. You get the vomiting of blood (don't worry, it's only blood-red dyes). Also crazy boots with five-inch soles and bigger heels. And instead of soft lights you get pulsating beams of laser light as well as a flame-eating act. Kiss is the kind of a pop group that you'd think was thought up by a mod Dr. Frankenstein. One record executive says, "They're big album sellers, and they're a big visual act."

The comic book monsters of rock record for Casablanca. Its members include singer-bassist

Gene Simmons (former Queens, N.Y. school teacher), singer-guitarist Ace Frenley (formerly in the liquor business), guitarist Paul Stanley, and drummer Peter Criss.

Their first gig was at a Queens, N.Y. nightclub, Coventry. In 1974 their first album was released. The pop press, anxious to write about something odd, started to write about them. Kiss visited the disc jockeys, worked the hype machine, and before long they had quite a following with their stage shows and heavy rock. The Kiss sound is the sound of super amplification with dozens of amplifiers and speakers. On tour they carry seven truckloads of audio equipment and a huge portable set. Gene Simmons says, "We're not making art, we're making rock and roll and rock and roll is a non-thinking music."

Phenomenally successful, they have had best-selling records, and have appeared in one TV film so far, *Kiss Meets the Phantom*. Kids seem to like their style of horror put-on. And pop fan magazines are always offering full-color posters of the group as an extra bonus feature. When they traveled to Japan in 1978 they were as popular as shrimp tempura.

In an NBC documentary, *In the Land of Hype and Glory*, Edward Newman analyzed Kiss this way: "In the frenzied world of rock, where the audiences are young and volatile, Kiss has found a simple formula for success: hit those audiences with such a barrage of gimmicks, stunts, and theatrics that they won't be able to forget you."

Besides recording as a group, each of the members of Kiss has put out solo albums and single records. Several of them have been very popular. Kiss LPs include: *Alive 11, Destroyer, Love Gun, Originals, Rock and Roll Over.* In 1978 an anthology of their numbers were put together called *Kiss—Double Platinum.* Each song on the record had told two million copies as singles. The deluxe set leaped up on the charts quickly. In 1979 Ace Frenley had a hit single on the charts, "New York Groove."

KC AND THE
SUNSHINE BAND

★

"I used to sell mangos, avocados, anything, just so I could go out and buy records," says Harry Casey of KC and the Sunshine Band. Buying pop records was his thing as a Florida teenager. After high school, he got odd jobs and took courses in business, math, speech, and music at Miami Dade Junior College. His first recording was for a rip-off company from Nashville and cost him $500. One of the songs he sang on it was "If You're Ever in Miami." Then he got a job with TK Tone Distributors, picking and packing records. There, he met Rick Finch, electronics whiz and bass-guitar player.

Together they formed a pop group that's been incredibly successful, KC and the Sunshine Band. In 1973 they cut their first single, "Blow Your Whistle." It's an interracial group that plays high-powered rock. Harry Casey is a potent singer and something to watch. Sometimes he dances like a whirling top, sometimes he shakes as if possessed. He is young and girls find him sexy and cute. "Harry Casey is a genuine rock hero," wrote the *Toronto Sun*.

The musical style favored by Harry and Rick is good-time music—infectious and catchy, with elements of soul and the Caribbean. The result, according to one fan magazine, is that they spread "sunshine all over the land." They record for T-K, the firm they originally worked for as pickers and packers.

Stereo Review has pointed out: "They are funky and tight. . . They have a combination that grabs black audiences and white teeny-boppers and country clubbers alike." It added that KC's instrumental sound is strongly influenced by Miami's distinctive cultural mix. "In a city whose population is more than half Cuban, salsa and other Latin sounds are everywhere—and so are West Indian."

Though Harry Casey gets most of the publicity, Rick Finch is equally important. Rick contributes heavily in all technical aspects of their studio work, right down to mixing and mastering. (He also collects tropical birds—has more than 50.)

Starting in 1973, success came rapidly. Casey and Rick wrote, arranged, produced, and performed on the first Sunshine Band record, "Blow Your Whistle." The group was then called KC and The Sunshine Junkanoo Band. The word "junkanoo" (a percussion-oriented sound from the Bahamian Islands), was too hard for people to catch on to, and the name was simplified down to KC and the Sunshine Band on their second release, a song called "Sound Your Funky Horn." Both singles were top-15 on the R & B charts in the United States. Casey was also in demand as a studio performer for recording engineer sessions for other producers at T-K.

In the spring of 1974 came George McCrae's "Rock Your Baby," a multi-million selling, international number-one record. KC and the Sunshine Band, in addition to their own recordings, are the musicians who backed George on his hit single and subsequent albums, with Casey and Rick writing and producing all of the material.

As record producers, songwriters, and recording artists, KC and Rick have made their mark. Sample LP: *KC and The Sunshine Band/Part Three.*

THE KNACK

They emerged out of the L.A. club circuit. In a field where the so-called "overnight success" usually comes only after years of failure, The Knacks drew crowds from the very start and landed a major label recording contract with Capitol in less than a year.

There is, however, a history that goes back to 1974 when the two songwriters of the group, Doug Feiger and Berton Averre began writing songs together (after meeting in an L.A. bar band). They made tapes of their songs and took them around. "Nobody wanted to hear about it. Nobody," recalls Feiger. Feiger had come to California from Detroit in 1971 with his band, Sky, and stayed in L.A. when the group broke up and the others went home.

When the songs didn't sell, Feiger tried unsuccessfully to start a video project. Then he landed a gig with a German synthesizer group, Triumph, and played bass with The Rats, who landed a recording date for which Feiger and Averre provided a punk song, "B.F.D."

Determined to form a group that would sing their songs, Feiger and Averre finally interested Bruce Gary, a much-in-demand drummer, in working up a demo. Gary brought in bass player Prescott Niles, whom he knew from playing in various bands in England, since Feiger wanted to play rhythm guitar and sing lead. Averre would play lead guitar and sing.

They rehearsed just six days before their first date at the Whiskey. They played on "spec" (no pay) for their first bookings, but once they played they mostly got asked back by such clubs as the Troubador, the Starwood, and the Sweetwater. After just six gigs they were playing to packed houses and just 14 weeks after forming they sold out the Starwood three nights in a row (1,000 people a night). Well-known rock stars like Ray Manzarek of The Doors, Stephen Stills, and Bruce Springsteen were making frequent guest appearances on stage with them. "Generally," explains Feiger, "they would come to the dressing room and ask to play with us."

Mike Chapman of Capitol, heard about The Knack from Los Angeles music journalist Harold Bronson, and the album *Get The Knack* was slated for recording after their tour of England and Europe. The album was recorded, mixed, and in the can in an amazing 11 days.

The band is full of energy. They have polish, and lead guitarist Berton Averre seems to like the nervy, high-end distorted sound George Harrison popularized with the Beatles. Bassist Prescott

Niles has a full, round sound, and drummer Bruce Gary tends to play like a sober Keith Moon. But the real reason for their "sound" is the songs, with a tough lyrical stance full of thwarted emotions: "If you let her go, she will break your ego and your heart" ("That's What the Little Girls Do"); and "she's gonna hurt you, don't ask me why ("Lucinda"). Most of their songs are about girls and love.

One theory afloat is that these four guys sat down about a year ago and proceded to manufacture commercial music that would realize their dreams of success.

"Truly," says Feiger," we didn't sit down and say, 'Let's dream up a marketing concept and go out and make a million dollars because we can't make it doing our 'art music.' To us rock and roll is not *art*. At best it's craft. We like to think we follow in a tradition of craftsmen. The people we loved were Bacharach and David, Lennon and McCartney, Brian Wilson, Phil Spector, Mann and Will, Gene Pitney, Paul Simon, Bob Dylan—people who took simple rock and roll music and put a little more craft into it."

Their second album, ... *but the little girls understand,* was released in February 1980.

KRIS
KRISTOFFERSON

He's a bearded, husky, country singer-songwriter, whose macho good looks have helped him in two careers: one in music and the other in films. Born in Brownsville, Texas, June 22, 1937, Kristofferson is a former Rhodes scholar and pilot. Kris has starred in eight motion pictures so far (musical and dramatic). In the commercially successful but artificial rock remake of *A Star Is Born* with Barbra Streisand, he played a fading rock star. In 1974 he married pop singer Rita Coolidge, but they have since separated.

Kris is a fair singer. He has a matter-of-fact, undramatic baritone. As a performer, he has been criticized. In a review of *Kris and Rita: Natural Act*, an LP he and his ex-wife did together, the *Village Voice* wrote: "K and R don't go out of their way to be interesting."

He shines mostly for his physical appeal and his

slangy poetic lyrics. As a lyricist he builds a lot of his words out of real experiences (which is what teachers of writing always suggest). For example, his hitchhiking days are depicted in "Me an' Bobby McGee." That was his first big hit (1969) recorded by Roger Miller and Janis Joplin. His other songs deal with trying to make it during painful personal crises such as "Help Me Make It Through the Night." An interest in an unusual island in the Pacific known for its stone heads (30 to 40 feet tall) led to his recent 1978 LP, *Easter Island.*

Literature has given him a sense of narrative and words. He tried to use everyday language in country rock songs. In Nashville's Music City he almost had to hide his education. As he once put it while guesting on *Saturday Night Live,* "Like a lotta you out there, I had a handicap. I was a college graduate with degrees in literature and creative writing and I couldn't get arrested."

Born into an Army family, his father was a major general. Kris picked up the guitar as a kid. He learned country songs in high school but he had no thought of music as a career. Literature seemed to be more his bag. He attended California's Pomona College, majoring in creative writing. He entered an *Atlantic Monthly* collegiate short story contest and won the top 4 of 20 prizes. He then went on to Oxford University for two years, then joined the Army where he became an officer.

Kris had an offer to teach literature at West Point when he stopped off at Nashville. He liked Nashville better and decided to break into the music business instead. He made contacts while working as a janitor at Columbia's recording studios, and bartending at a local bar, The Tally Ho Tavern.

Now film scripts pile up on his doorstep. A prominent Hollywood actor, he has had important roles in *Alice Doesn't Live Here Anymore, Pat Garrett and Billy the Kid, Blume in Love, The Sailor That Fell From Grace With The Sea* and *Semi-Tough* (about football players).

He cut his first album in 1971, *The Silver Tongued Devil and I.* That same year he recorded a second album, *Me and Bobby McGee.* So far his discography lists 11 LPs and 13 singles.

LED ZEPPELIN

When the Yardbirds dissolved in 1968, guitarist Jimmy Page and long-time musician friend John Paul Jones talked about forming their own band. They found Robert Plant on the recommendation of drummer B.J. Wilson, and Plant suggested John "Bonzo" Bonham as drummer. They called themselves The New Yardbirds and toured Scandanavia. When, shortly afterward, they were going to be recording for Atlantic, they decided to come up with a name of their own and "Led Zeppelin" was born.

Around this time they made up their minds to try making it in the U.S. rather than in their native Great Britain. Their first album, *Led Zeppelin I*, was released in 1969 and became the standard for heavy rock for the next decade.

Lead guitarist and producer/arranger for the hard-rock band, Jimmy Page, was born in Middlesex, England, in 1945. He was 14 when he got his first guitar, a Grazzioso. His early influences were people like Johnny Weeks, and blues guitarist B.B.

King. For two years he stopped playing and went to an art college. Then he started going to the Marquee Club in London to jam. There he was heard and asked to make a record. That began his professional career.

John Paul Jones is Led Zeppelin's solid, animated bassist. This Londoner's father was a piano player and bandleader. John had only one lesson on the bass and says he was mainly influenced by Charles Mingus. The best way to learn bass, he says, is to switch on the radio and play along with whatever comes on. He played piano when he was younger, but found out the rock and roll band at school needed either a drummer or bassist and decided in favor of the bass—easier to get on the bus. His first instrument was a Dallas bass guitar.

Singer-lyricist Robert Plant is the idol of fans and never wrote a song before Led Zeppelin. He is witty, intellectually curious, and an amateur historian. Plant, son of a Birmingham, England, civil engineer, was supposed to have studied accounting at Cambridge but was lured away by black blues music into bohemian circles in Birmingham. One of the bands he discovered in the mid-'60s was the Band of Joy, whose drummer was John Bonham, another local boy, John ("Bonzo"), according to his bio, was unpopular in clubs around his hometown because he played too loudly. For the Led Zeppelin, he provides a no-frills, straight-away, steady beat. He is fond of machines with wheels.

In 1969 Led Zeppelin's first album, *Led Zeppelin I*, became a critical failure, but a commercial hit, and "Good Times Bad Times" was a success. *Led*

Zeppelin II gained them star status, but still not with critics. *Led Zeppelin III*, in 1970, gave them their second major hit single, "The Immigrant-Song." Critics still booed, but fans bought it. *Led Zeppelin IV* a year later emphasized hard rock and included "Stairway to Heaven," considered one of their best songs.

In 1973 they toured America, smashing all box office records, and even critics began to mellow. *Houses of the Holy* was the next release and disappointed both fans and critics, but still achieved platinum status. In 1974 they formed their own label, Swan Song (distributed by Atlantic), and produced a two-record set, *Physical Graffiti.* The public rushed to buy it and the critics still complained. Later that year, Plant's injuries due to a car accident restricted the group's activities until 1976 when they came up with *Presence* and released film footage of a 1973 concert at Madison Square Garden which they called *The Song Remains the Same.* Then things caved in for them in 1977 when John Bonham was convicted of attacking aides of promoter Bill Graham, and Plant's five-year-old son, Karac, died of a mysterious infection, leaving him mourning.

Now they are back with a new album, *In Through the Out Door,* containing seven original compositions and developing an awareness of contemporary rock trends.

LORETTA LYNN

Loretta's fascinating, best-selling autobiography, *Coal Miner's Daughter*, has been made into a wonderful film. It's quite a story. Petite, 5"2½" Loretta Webb was born on April 14, 1935, in Butcher's Hollow, a few miles from the Van Lear, Kentucky, coal mine where her father worked. From a big family, she helped her mother care for the younger children—seven brothers and sisters. Each day Loretta walked several miles through rural Kentucky to go to school. School was a one-room affair. Loretta made a little extra pocket money for doing chores at school.

As a teenager, she sang in church. At 14, she married a man she met at a church pie supper, O.V. Lynn, a former coalminer in his twenties, who had his eye on becoming a rodeo rider. They picked up and moved to Custer, Washington.

"I was starved for anything from back home, especially music," Loretta once revealed in an interview in BMI's *World of Music*. One night her husband said there'd be some country music at

the Custer Grange Hall, where rural people met. They went. During the social her husband got up on a table and told the audience Loretta could "out sing" anybody. However, Loretta didn't get her chance that night, but later on she got on a local radio program. Nervous and scared, Loretta conquered her fears and sang songs from back home, songs she had sung to her baby on lonely nights.

Her first hit record was on a small label, Zero Records, "I'm a Honky Tonk Girl." This gave her quite a push and she became known in and around Nashville. In the early '60s she was signed by Decca Records (which later turned into MCA Records). She's still with MCA. Today she is one of the top country stars, singing, playing guitar, and heading up her own band.

These days, the poor miner's daughter who was named after the movie actress Loretta Young, is wealthy. The sweet-faced brunette owns a big ranch in Hurricane Mills, Tennessee. She's also involved financially with successful rodeo shows through her husband. She has a Nashville office that takes care of her singing tours and music publishing.

She's an appealing performer. As a songwriter, she uses homey rural speech to sketch observations on love and life. Her hits reflect this: "You Ain't Woman Enough (to Take My Man)," "Don't Come A-Drinkin' (With Lovin' on Your Mind)," "The World of Forgotten People." She's also written "Coal Miner's Daugher," a powerful song based on personal experiences so grimly realistic that it makes you almost taste coal dust.

Today Loretta Lynn is bigger than ever. She does TV, cuts records, a plays big country fairs, and even nightclubs as a Las Vegas headliner. Lately she's been recording a lot of songs that touch on the women's movement, including "You've Come a Long Way, Baby." In 1979 MCA did a little checking and reported that Loretta has produced 38 albums so far. Among them: *I Remember, Out of My Head.*

MELISSA MANCHESTER

"I grew up in New York City," she says, "and when I went to school I was on the street. We ran in a pack. But I always felt out of sync, slight out of time. I was slightly leaning toward fantasy to survive school. My report card always said, 'The kid has tremendous potential. Should work hard.'"

In her teen years, she auditioned and got into the prestigious High School of Performing Arts on West 46th Street in Manhattan's theatrical district. "Missy," as friends call her, seemed to be in sync in show business. While going to this special public high school that trains actors, singers, and dancers, she made the rounds and got assignments to write songs and to record commercial jingles. With her foot in the door, Melissa has gone on to stardom. She guests a lot on TV, does commercials (for Memorex), and has had a number of hit singles and albums.

Her bushy, flowing brunette hair, that's sometimes done in ringlets, sits on top of a Shirley
Temple-ish face. She's no militant feminist, but
she has participated in a variety of women's-only
events, including a workshop on songwriting at
a Women's Music Festival in Champagne, Illinois.
She sings, plays piano, writes music and lyrics.

Melissa mixes rock, gospel, show-tune type
songs, soft whispers, and dramatic autobiography.
Lots of personal thoughts run through her lyrics.
Melissa writes most of the songs she records but
she also does songs by others, including her record
producer, Vini Poncia and with collaborator Carole Bayer Sager. Her singles include "Home to
Myself" and "Bright Eyes." She reads a great deal.
Years ago, she was deep into the novels of John
Fowles, plays of Tennessee Williams, and "special
philosophers." She puts down her thoughts in a
journal, which often turns into songs.

"Ultimately," she once told Associated Press,
"the theme of most of my music is not to
be a cockeyed optimist, but the feeling of self-
affirmation. The entitlement to one's existence
no matter what it is, and the ability to be. Self-
affirmation."

She grew up in a musical household in the Bronx
and later, Manhattan. Her father, David, is a bas-
soonist with the Metropolitan Opera Orchestra.
Her mother, Ruth, is a dress designer who has
fashioned several of Melissa's costumes. Her first
two albums were *Home to Myself* and *Bright Eyes*,
both on Bell Records. (Bell later became Arista).
Arista's top man Clive Davis helped match her
with producer Vini Poncia. In 1975 she had a

smash single, "Midnight Blue." In '79 she had another big single, "Don't Cry Out Loud." Larry Brezner is her husband and is in the business. He is personal manager for her and other performers. They live in California.

Her LPs include: *Don't Cry Out Loud, Singin', Melissa.*

CHUCK MANGIONE

Can you imagine a flügelhorn player as head of
a top pop group? There is one, and he's Chuck
Mangione, a native of Rochester, New York, born
Nov. 29, 1940. Mangione was musically preco-
cious. At 13, he started jamming with jazz great
Dizzy Gillespie. Dizzy was so impressed with the
teenager that he gave him, as a gift, one of his odd-
shaped, bent trumpets. Later, Chuck went on to
play with the Jazz Brothers (with his brother Gap).
He also played with other jazz groups—those of
Maynard Ferguson, Art Blakely, and Keith Jarrett.
Today he is one of the few jazz-type performers
making it in the world of rock.

The Mangione sound is broad, lush melody,
both lyrical and warm. His tunes, according to one
critic, are long on symmetry, built on easy inter-
vals. His harmonies are easy to follow. His tempos
are comfortable, middle-of-the-road. He uses

strings and horns with taste, also touches of Latin-American music.

The lean, mustached Mangione often wears black cowboy-type hats. Chuck initially recorded for Mercury; now his work is on A & M Records. Besides playing flügelhorn (which produces soft mellow sounds), he plays piano and composes words and music. He has toured a lot and is the recipient of two Grammy Award nominations. He is also a former teacher and director of jazz ensembles at Rochester's famed Eastman School of Music.

Mangione hates music labels such as rock, contemporary pop, jazz, or fusion rock. "Music is either good or bad," he says. "Where music is honest and full of love, labels aren't important." He adds, "What I want to do is create music that is important and meaningful, that says something about the world we live in today, to listeners both young and not so young. And just as important, I want to write music that challenges the players who are performing it."

One of Mangione's most typical and winning LPs is the touching *Land of Dreams*. In 1976 his theme, "Bellavia" won a Grammy nomination. They used his theme, "Chase the Clouds Away" for the 1976 Olympic telecasts, and he provided much of the music for ABC's telecast of the 1980 Winter Olympics.

In 1978 Mangione's star rose higher than his highest notes. He had a Top-10 singles hit, "Feels So Good," and a best-selling LP, the soundtrack for the film, *Children of Sanchez*. (He wrote the music.) In '78, too, he won a "Georgie" from the

American Guild of Variety Artists (AGVA) as best instrumental artist. Other co-winners were funny-man Steve Martin and the Bee Gees. Worth noting is that Mangione and Co. is one of the few popular groups that lean heavily on instrumentals.

Chuck on LP: *Land of Dreams, Quartet, Friends and Love, Best of Chuck Mangione* (Mercury records); *Bellavia, Feels So Good, Chase Clouds, Children of Sanchez* (A & M Records).

BARRY MANILOW

Barry Manilow sees nothing wrong with romantic music. "The hard rock critics run down and feel uncomfortable with soft, romantic pop. They prefer funky and complicated lyrics that are 'profound' and the driving big beat sound. They are uncomfortable with simplicity."

He's gone with his brand of soft, romantic pop and succeeded. A believer in melody, he has managed to make it big with a succession of big-selling singles and albums. He records for Arista. His single "I Write the Songs," sold more than three million. In 1978, a double album, *Barry Manilow's Greatest Hits,* went on sale. Within five days it sold two million copies at $14 each.

The singer-pianist-songwriter was born June 17, 1946 in Brooklyn, N.Y. From ages 7 to 12 he studied the accordion and played pop standards and Latin-American favorites like "Tico Tico." He went to Eastern District H.S. (a rough high school), where he was pushed around quite a bit. Once, his stepfather took him to hear ace baritone saxophonist, Gerry Mulligan. That blew his mind. From accordion he went on to piano. On the radio, he discovered show tunes—Gershwin, Rodgers and Hart, Cole Porter, Lerner and Loewe. He never thought too much about pop music until the Beatles conquered America. He went one year to City College, majoring in advertising. That didn't work out. Later he enrolled at the New York College of Music, and still later, briefly at Juilliard. "I'd always known I was musical. I was just scared to do it to earn a living," he says.

At 18, he had a job in a mailroom in CBS in New York. That led to arranging assignments with a talent TV show, *Call Back.* Later he joined up with a girl and did a two-person act, but it didn't get anywhere. During those early days, Barry also sang musical jingles for "Big Mac" and other products (Band-Aids, etc.). He also wrote a musical melodrama that's still being produced. *The Drunkard.*

His big break came when he was down and got a job playing piano at the Continental Baths in New York. There he met singer Bette Midler, also down on her luck. Barry accompanied her and did arrangements. Later on, Bette got hot and Barry went with her on the road as musical director-arranger-accompanist; he even went on as "opening act." He did so well that it led to a contract with Arista Records, a young record company just starting out. In 1975 he cut his first single smash, "Mandy." In 1977 his *Barry Manilow Special* won an Emmy Award.

Not handsome or glamorous, Barry has ordinary features. He has bronzed hair and a kind of chunky figure. His loyal fans are very loyal and think he's handsome and if you differ, watch out. He enjoys backgammon, Scrabble, and offbeat food. He has a lively beagle named Bagel.

His hit singles: "It's a Miracle," "Could It Be Magic," "Tryin' to Get the Feeling," "This One's for You," "Weekend in New England," "Looks Like We Made It," and "Daybreak." Barry on LP: *Barry Manilow Live.*

BOB MARLEY

★

Reggae is sort of a black pop/folk music from the Caribbean. It features vocals and guitars, plus the percussive knocking of oil drums and pans. The oil drums are hand-hammered to produce a wide variety of sounds. The rhythms and accents, the structure of the lyrics go way back to Africa, the roots of the black population of the Islands. The English lyrics are close to colloquial speech, mixed with mysticism, and resembling folk poetry. One of the biggest reggae stars who has also established quite a following in the U.S. is Bob Marley.

He's from the ghettos of Kingston, the capitol of the island of Jamaica. Some of his records have appeared on Trojan Records, some on Island Records. His songs are bold, have sharp touches of humor, and rap the establishment. It comes out of a poor black's attitude toward the law, nature, and love. There's also a lot of belief in Rastafarianism, a home-grown religion with touches of the supernatural. Musically, he mixes up reggae with rock, soul, and other contemporary influences. His brand of Caribbean pop, wrote one critic in *New Times*, is "melodically appealing, rhythmically subtle, and commercially viable."

The singer-guitarist-songwriter is considered Jamaica's musical genius. He has been written up by *People*, *Time*, and *Rolling Stone* as a global superstar who sells a lot of records and is capable of drawing big crowds, whether it be in Jamaica, New York, or London.

He surfaced as a pop personality in 1964. His backup group has had many changes of name and many changes of personnel. Once they were known as the Wailers, then the Wailing Rudeboys, the Wailing Wailers, and Wailing Soul. His early group broke up because some of its members thought that Marley was getting too much attention and publicity. Despite internal bickering, Marley is a force, and his records have been listened to with much appreciation by such groups as the Rolling Stones. Marley's popularity has led many American pop stars to recording reggae-flavored numbers.

He's cut records in Jamaica, the U.S., and in London. One LP he made in London was taped "live" at the Lyceum Theatre. (There is a large Caribbean population in London.) Called *Bob Marley: Live*, it contained such tunes as "Trenchtown," "No Woman, No Cry," "I Shot the Sherrif," "Lively Up Yourself," and "Get Up and Stand Up." His songs are often militant, prodding people to stand up for their rights.

A beloved idol in Jamaica, once he returned to Kingston after a period of being away, he was met at the airport by the prime minister of that country and by 5,000 joyous fans.

His LPs include: *Rasta Revolution*, *African Herbsman*, *Burnin' Kaya*.

PAUL
McCARTNEY

★

The number-one Beatle today is Paul McCartney. He is the most active, most successful of them all. Since the breakup of the fab four, he has continued to write, give concerts, and record. In a recent edition of *The Guinness Book of World Records*, it was reported that Paul is the number-one Gold Album King, with 59 of them so far; 43 as the result of his Beatle days and 16 with his Wings group.

The British pop millionaire is married to a New York photographer, Linda Eastman. She also sings, plays keyboard, and writes songs. Paul has written a song about this daughter of a show business attorney, "The Lovely Linda." Mr. and Mrs. McCartney have two children, one from Linda's former marriage.

Singer-songwriter, lefthanded guitarist-keyboard player, James Paul McCartney was born in

Liverpool, England, June 18, 1942. Father a cotton salesman. He met John Lennon at 15. Together with George Harrison and Ringo Starr he formed perhaps the most successful and creative group ever. Their songs from the '60s that emerged in *Revolver, Sergeant Pepper's Lonely Hearts Club Band, Abbey Road* were looked upon as modern classics.

Paul's an effective instrumentalist, painstaking record producer, singer, and talented vocal arranger. A gifted songwriter (with John Lennon and alone) his writing covers sweet ballads ("Michelle"), rocking material, teenage silliness, chant-like songs ("Give Peace a Chance"), and avantgarde items that resemble free association experiments in literature and poetry. Alone he has crafted songs for a growing list of albums with Wings, a group he organized.

Because he can afford it, Paul does things in style. Production of an LP of his can start in Northern England, at his home in the Scottish hills, continue on in the Virgin Islands, and conclude somewhere else. His record sessions are often lengthy. Things are gone over and over and over. When that happens, he often makes the studio a second home. Once, for example, he was working at England's EMI Abbey Road Studio 2. So Paul and Linda made it homier by bringing in plants in pots, chairs that grouped around a café table topped by a beach umbrella. And when the studio work continued on to late November, Christmas decorations were put up.

Beatlemania still exists in the form of books *(Apple to the Core)* re-issues of Beatle LPs, and even a successful stage show with Beatle look-alikes that had a long run on Broadway and across the country called *Beatlemania*. But Paul likes to stress what he is doing now, rather than what happened in the legendary past.

Early in '79 Paul broke away from his long relationship with Capitol Records to sign up with Columbia. It was reported to be one of the biggest deals in disc history; bigger than contracts signed with Elton John and Stevie Wonder. And in March, CBS-TV telecast a 90-minute concert mixed with interviews on a program called *Wings Over the World*. LPs featuring Paul McCartney in stage two of his career include: *Band on the Run, McCartney Ram, Wings Over America, London Town*. He also won a Grammy for Best Original Score for Motion Picture on TV for *Let It Be*.

MEAT LOAF

The wild man of rock. He has a beer-barrel belly and tips the scale at 200 pounds, sometimes 300. "I got the nickname 'Meat loaf' in Texas, playing football, and it just stuck," he once told *Hit Parader*. "Eventually, it became so common to me that I called myself that. I joined unions and things like that with that name."

On stage he is an unbelievable, outrageous spectacle. At a concert in New York's Palladium, he stormed out like a used car salesman, spotting three potential customers. He prowled the stage, and as he sang he stripped off his tuxedo like a madman, while trying to push back his stringy, sweaty hair. He stomped like a Texas longhorn.

Meat Loaf has a powerful, gritty voice, rooted in gospel and rhythm and blues. His real name (kept secret for a while for publicity reasons) is Marvin Lee Aday. Born in Dallas, Sept. 27, 1947, into a family of Southern gospel singers, Meat Loaf built quite a reputation singing in rock bands on the West Coast. He was the lead singer with the

hard-rock guitarist Ted Nugent on *Free for All*, a platinum record. He also worked on and off-Broadway in *Hair* and a satirical revue, *The National Lampoon Show*. The Texan has also been seen in that cult film, *The Rocky Horror Show*. In it he portrayed the singing, crazy Eddie, a '50s type grocery delivery boy with one defect—half of his brain had been removed.

Called "a singing giant" Meat Loaf works with a partner, Jim Steadman, who plays keyboards. (Often the two of them front a small combo. Occasionally Meat Loaf performs with a female singer.) The rock press generally has looked upon Meat Loaf favorably. However, *Variety* had criticized his musical approach. Reviewing his Palladium concert, the entertainment weekly wrote: "The screaming which he [Meat Loaf] palmed off as singing was excessive, but his fans seemed to love it."

The material Meat Loaf does is by Jim Steadman. Jim's got a wild fantasy-type mind with a taste for creepy horror and the occult. "I've always been fascinated by the supernatural," says Steadman. "And I always felt that rock was the perfect idiom for it."

Oddly enough, Steadman also composes very romantic ballads. Meat Loaf sings them with a soaring, driving intensity that resembles opera arias. Incidentally, their debut album, *Bat Out of Hell*, (Cleveland International/Epic) proved to be a five-million seller.

Physically, Meat Loaf is big, and Jim is small and compact. Steadman grew up in the glazed and disoriented world of rock and roll in Claremont,

California. Later, he went east to Long Island. Jim and Marvin joined forces after they both appeared in *The National Lampoon Show*, which had material in it kidding rock and roll stars. They got along so well together they decided to become a team. Jim writes the songs and does the arranging, and Meat Loaf sings them in a distinctive meat and potatoes style that's half put-on and half pure primal energy. Somebody has called it "Revved-Up Rock."

BETTE MIDLER

Five-foot one-inch Bette got discovered in a steambath, the Continental, in Manhattan. The kooky singer was hired to entertain patrons wrapped in big bath towels. People heard her and thought she was hotter than a sauna and equally as refreshing. Her accompanist, incidentally, was Barry Manilow. You can see her in a drier situation, the hit movie, *The Rose.*

Daughter of a house painter, she was born in Paterson, New Jersey, Dec. 1, 1945. "The Divine Miss M," as she became known later, was named after Bette Davis. Later on, the family moved to Hawaii where she grew up on Oahu. After high school, she attended the University of Hawaii. While going to college she also worked sorting pineapple slices in a food packing plant, and as a secretary.

In the beginning she wanted to be an actress. Her first credit was a bit part in the film, *Hawaii.* Later she moved to Los Angeles, and then to New

York. Here she became a singer, out of necessity, by trying out for a job with *Fiddler on the Roof*. She auditioned and landed a role in the chorus of the New York cast. She stayed with the show for three years. She continued performing as a singer in the off-Broadway musical, *Salvation*, and in Catskills resorts.

Nothing much happened after that. In 1970 she was very low when she got a call to sing at the health club. There she was discovered amidst the heat, the steam, and the chlorine-scented pool. Soon the papers were talking about this madcap singer who had a fantastic range: she could do straight pop, show tunes, soul, blues, and even sang swing tunes such as those made famous by the Andrews Sisters in the 1940s ("Boogie Woogie Bugle Boy From Company B").

Along with her voice, she had something else— a sense of wacky comedy. She is both a singer and comedienne, similar to the early Barbra Streisand. In a review of her work, *The New York Times* once wrote: "Her raffishness seems to come from a deep well of merriment; she has a gaiety and a sweetness one seldom finds in a comic, man or woman. And there's nothing she can't sing. Rock. Blues. Songs from the forties."

She's easygoing and willing to be on. Not long ago, there was a blizzard, and she couldn't get out of her hotel to get to the auditorium in which she was scheduled to perform. So Bette gave an impromptu performance in the hotel coffee shop for her appreciative snowbound guests.

Quite overpowering, while guesting on *The*

Carol Burnett Show not long ago, she outdid Carol with her comic "takes." Besides TV, nightclubs, and concerts, she has made quite a few recordings on Atlantic. These include: *The Divine Miss M, Broken Blossom, Live at Last.*

STEVE MILLER

A blues-rock-guitarist-songwriter from Milwaukee, Wisconsin, Steve Miller records on Capitol Records. He started in music when he was 4½, just a little bigger than the guitar his father bought him. The tot had his own way of playing the guitar—he hit it. Then a family friend came for a visit, singer-guitarist Mary Ford, who cut many hit records with Les Paul. She showed him how to play simple chords.

Not long after, the family moved to Dallas. As he grew up, Steve stuck with music and the guitar. He even formed small bands in high school to play at dances. When he was 17, until the time he was 21, he jobbed around from Texas to Wisconsin to Chicago and back to Texas. During this period he also attended college, majoring in comparative literature. On his own, he majored in the blues. Finally, he dropped academic studies to concentrate on music.

In Chicago he sat in and played with some of the blues greats—Muddy Waters, Otis Rush, Buddy

Guy, and others. With a musician friend, Barry Goldberg, he formed the Goldberg-Miller Blues Band, which made a bit of a stir before it sank. At 23 he put together the Steve Miller Band, which did very well in San Francisco. On the West Coast, he and his band played the blues-rock circuit—the Matrix, the Avalon, and Fillmore West. Gradually, they became one of the hottest bands in the "underground."

Hollywood then tapped him to supply music for the soundtrack of a United Artists film, *Revolution*. For the film, Steve wrote three songs. A little later on, he played the Monterey Pop Festival, and this led to Capitol Records signing him up.

His first album, produced by Miller himself, was *Children of the Future*, recorded in England. *Rolling Stone* praised it, and *Eye* magazine said, "Watch out for this big talent." Through the years, he has gone on to greater success. Capitol describes his style as "rock with the basic drive and raunchiness of the blues. Steve uses electronics technology with subtlety and taste, and with it achieves lovely and ethereal effects."

Early in 1979 his LP, *The Steve Miller Band's Greatest Hits 1974–1978*, reached the best-seller charts. It included such single hits as "The Joker," "Fly Like an Eagle," "Swingtown," "Jet Airliner," "Take the Money and Run." In a review of his "hits album" *Newsday* wrote: "Miller's best songs embody the virtues of clean, unambitious pop music, strong on melody with a few tasty fills and a minimum of embellishment."

Steve on LP: *Book of Dreams, Greatest Hits, 1974–1978*.

LIZA MINNELLI

Liza with a Z. She loves speed, flash, glitter, discos, dancing. When she appeared in *The Act* on Broadway, Liza worked very hard. It was practically a one-woman show. She was on most of the time, singing and dancing. Yet when the curtain went down, after 2½ hours of performing, this wide-eyed girl with the boyish hairdo would relax by dancing hour after hour at a New York disco, Studio 54.

Not a big record-seller, she's heard mostly on show music albums. Among her LP's are cast albums of *Cabaret* (the million-selling album of the film soundtrack), *Flora the Red Menace*, *The Act*, and an LP based on her award-winning TV show, *Liza With a Z*. While people with far less talent sell millions of records, Liza, nevertheless, is one of the great figures in American musical comedy. She stands close to and alongside such personalities as Mary Martin, Ethel Merman, and her own mother, the late Judy Garland.

The talented singer-actress was born Mar. 12, 1946. Her father is Vincente Minnelli, the film director of such screen musicals as *An American In Paris*, *Funny Face*, and the classic *Meet Me in St. Louis*. Of course, Judy Garland is a tough act to follow. But Liza has, with distinction. She is now a star on her own. Her name on a marquee is pretty much box office magic in the U.S., England, and elsewhere. In her brief career she has done Broadway, clubs, theater, TV, and even straight movies. She did a marvelous acting job as the overly possessive girl student, Pookie Adams, in *The Sterile Cuckoo*. For this sensitive portrayal she won an Academy Award nomination. For *Cabaret*, she won the Oscar for Best Actress.

In the musical department, she's a great belter, but she can also sing quiet songs. "Her voice," once wrote Clive Barnes, the *New York Post* drama critic, "has that special poignancy that all great cabaret performers seem to have, and her personality takes off like a rocket."

Not too tall, she gives a tall appearance, because she moves so well. She's a highly talented dancer, and when she does special TV appearances such as a recent one on the Tony Awards, she was pure wham bang fusion.

Liza made her professional debut at the age of 12 on a Gene Kelly TV special. Even then one reviewer remarked, "She managed to radiate the kind of magic of which stars are made." Later on she did well in a small role in an off-Broadway production of *Best Foot Forward*. All the time she was fighting the prejudice that matched her against her mother, which was most unfair. Today, though, she is a great star.

Liza on LP: *Cabaret* (soundtrack), *The Act*, *New York, New York* (soundtrack).

JONI MITCHELL

Creator of more than 100 songs that resemble little, short stories. Many are thoughtful and moody in a folklike vein, based on her own experiences and travels. The Canadian-born singer-songwriter now records for Asylum Records. Possessing an austere face and a sweet, cool sound, Joni is restless. Recently, she left the luxury of a fabulous Spanish-style Bel Air home in California (so beautiful it was featured in *Architectural Digest*) to take a loft in So Ho. So Ho is in lower New York City, where many artists, musicians, and chic young people live in remodeled factory-lofts that cost $700 a month and up.

Born Nov. 7, 1943, in McLeod, Alberta, Canada, Joni attended public schools in Saskatoon, Saskatchewan and, bent on a career as a commercial artist, enrolled in the Alberta College of Art in Calgary. Just to pass the time, she took along a ukulele. After mastering some chords and a few traditional ballads, she found she could earn extra money by singing, and got her first job in a coffee house called the Depression. As time went on she found she enjoyed singing more than painting, and decided to make a trek to the Mariposa Folk Festival in Ontario, a three-day trip east on the Canadian Pacific. On the way she wrote her first song, a blues number called "Day After Day," timed to the clacking of train wheels on steel rails.

And she didn't return to Alberta. Instead she found work in half a dozen Toronto coffee houses and continued to write songs. In Toronto she met Chuck Mitchell and married him in June of 1965. A year later she went with him to live in Detroit, but the marriage was dissolved soon after that. Joni continued appearing in Detroit clubs, then came to New York where Reprise's Andy Wickham discovered and signed her.

In her spare time, Joni paints, collects Navajo baskets. She also has a one-room cabin in Canada. "I simply hired a stone mason and we built it ourselves. I like to go there and stay a couple of weeks and get recycled," she says.

She is best known for "Both Sides Now" (a contemporary classic) that talks about looking at problems, and ideas from different points of view.

Joni on LP: *Blue, Clouds, Court and Spark, For the Roses, Joni Mitchell, Ladies of the Canyon, Miles of Isles, Don Juan's Reckless Daughter*, and others.

EDDIE MONEY

"My family has seen me go through so many stages it's outrageous," says Eddie Money, whose real name is Eddie Mahoney. As a kid he wanted to be a cowboy, and secondly a rock star. But the men in Eddie Mahoney's Irish family generally joined "the force," the New York Police Department. In fact, Eddie himself was tracked into a career in law enforcement. Born in Brooklyn, N.Y., he enrolled at the N.Y. Police Academy after high school. But while he was studying policework by day, he played and sang with rock and roll groups. He also hung out with rock people at night, a fact that his "strict" family wasn't crazy about.

Eventually, the young man had to choose between the two fields. It was painful. He decided that he had to break away. He packed his surfboard ("What you think, we didn't surf on Long Island?") and his Dylan albums and moved to Berkeley, California. There he fronted a group called The Rockets. It made a little bit of splash in and around the Bay Area. He even got a big part in a one-man play, *Back Tracks*, that was produced in San Francisco in 1977. In it he played a 90-year-old former rock star who becomes "the last man on earth." Then he was spotted by Bill Graham, rock concert producer, former impressario of Fillmore East. His evaluation: "Eddie Money has it all; not only can he sing, write and play, but he's also a natural performer, and he's very, very hungry."

Graham signed on to be his personal manager. Eddie soon ceased to be very, very hungry and instead became very, very hot. The first two singles from his debut album on Columbia Records, "Baby, Hold On" and "Two Tickets to Paradise," soared up the charts in the most rapid possible succession. He toured Europe twice, appearing on Spanish, French, and German television, and crashed the Dutch Top-10 with "Baby, Hold On." His album was certified platinum in Canada. Back home, American concert audiences—including many which numbered over 50,000 when he opened for such formidable acts as the Rolling Stones, The Eagles, and Fleetwood Mac—tendered him standing ovations. His singularly stirring stage manner is the quintessence of sexy, sweat-drenched rock and roll passion.

Today Money is coining money. Early in 1979 he hit the Top-10 charts once again with his second LP, *Life for the Taking*. His lyrics revolve about two topics: the man of action ("The Gambler") and sex. He sings in a gravelly voice. His music is tuneful hard rock.

ANNE MURRAY

Her voice is mellow, easy to listen to. She's a pretty, 5'6", petite blonde Canadian singer who records for Capitol. Anne was born on June 20, 1946. She was raised in the mining town of Springfield, Nova Scotia, with five brothers. As a teenager, she loved athletics. In fact, her dream was to become a physical education teacher. But she also enjoyed music, particularly singing. "We all took piano lessons," she once told *Song Hits*. "I was singing as long as I can remember, but at 15 I began taking singing lessons from Karen Mills, who had sung with symphonies. She lived about 50 miles away, so every Saturday morning, I would make the trip on the bus at seven-thirty in the morning and there was no return bus until seven-thirty at night. I did that for two years and then another year while I was going to Mount St. Vincent College in Halifax.

Later Anne transferred to the University of New Brunswick. In Halifax, the big city there, she got on summer TV and in 1975 married a TV producer, William Langstroth. Singing as a career seemed risky, so she took physical education. She taught health education for a year at a high school on Prince Edward Island. Meanwhile she continued to sing on local Canadian TV. That led to cutting some records for a small Canadian label, Arc. Her first LP was *What About Me?* Capitol (the Canadian Division) liked it, and soon they recorded an album with her.

Her first release in the mid-seventies was a fantastic hit, "Snowbird." It turned out to be a global hit, and went gold in several countries. With that single Anne became the first Canadian female artist to get a gold record in the U.S.

Anne's other single hits include: "Danny's Song," "Love Song," "You Won't See Me," "He Thinks I Still Care," and "Son of a Rotten Gambler." She also has several Top-10 albums.

Her voice is pleasant, not strident. It goes well with sentimental songs. The Canadian songbird has sung frequently on CBC (Canadian Broadcasting Company) specials and programs, as well as on U.S. TV. She sticks pretty close to a semi-sweet form of country, but she also does soft rock. In another LP, *Let's Keep It That Way*, she even did a song with a reggae Caribbean rhythm, "Hold Me Tight." She's also done an album for children for TV's *Sesame Street*.

Anne lives in Toronto with her husband and two children. People who meet her are immediately struck by her warmth, openness, and honesty. She's won the Canadian Grammy (The Juno) five times during the 1970s as "Best Female Vocalist." She's also collected Grammy Awards from the U.S. and English honors too.

Anne on LP: *New Kind of Feeling, Snowbird, Love Song.*

WILLIE NELSON

A current pop idol is Willie Nelson, the singer-songwriter-guitarist from the Southwest. For about 20 years he sang his heart out in clubs and honky tonks around Austin, Texas. He wasn't famous but he was a familiar figure down there in his tennis shoes, sweatband, and off-and-on-again beard. In 1976 he exploded and won three awards at the annual Country Music Association Awards Show. In 1976 he also got a Grammy for "Blue Eyes Cryin' in the Rain," the "Country Single of the Year." Willie's been named to the Hall of Fame by the Nasville Songwriters Association. In 1978 five of his albums were among the top country music sellers.

Of his singing style, Willie says: "Actually, the way I sing isn't all that hard. It's phrasing. Sinatra's been phrasing for years; a lot of pop singers have. It's just that nobody in country music in those days was doing it. But I couldn't imitate anybody else."

Willie Nelson was born in Abbott, a tiny town

in north central Texas, on April 30, 1933. His musical career began over thirty years ago playing rhythm guitar with a Bohemian polka band one night. His grandparents, who raised him in the latter years of The Great Depression, earned mail-order music degrees. Willie used to watch them practice by lantern light in the evenings until he could play his first few chords on a guitar. This was Willie's only "formal" music training.

In 1950 after a short hitch in the Air Force, Willie set up housekeeping with a new bride in Waco. He played and sang in the area when he could. He supported his family (which soon included a daughter, Lana) by peddling vacuum cleaners, encyclopedias, and Bibles. Then he got a job as a disc jockey at a San Antonio radio station. In the next few years he worked at radio stations in Fort Worth, Houston, and for a while, even Oregon—and sang nights and weekends in nearby honky tonks.

In 1972 he moved back to Texas and started to build up his career as a singer as well as songwriter. These days he performs at college campuses, the Hollywood Bowl, as well as honky tonks and outdoor festivals.

Along that rugged uphill road, Willie started writing songs, sometimes scribbling lyrics on napkins, envelopes, and paper sacks. Famous songs which he wrote: "Hello, Walls," "Night Life," "Good Hearted Woman" and "Funny How Time Slips Away." (In April '79 it was reported that they're making a movie based on Willie's song, "Red Headed Stranger.")

A man of deep country music roots, Willie also

is a great admirer of the better Tin Pan Alley songs and Broadway show music by Irving Berlin and George Gershwin. Most rock and country people look down at this form of pop. Willie loves it. A recent LP, *Stardust*, is a Columbia album containing such non-country songs as "Someone to Watch Over Me," "Georgia on my Mind," "Blue Skies," "All of Me," and the title song.

Willie on LP: *Red Headed Stranger, Troublemaker, To Lefty From Willie, Wanted: The Outlaws, Waylon and Willie, Stardust.*

OLIVIA NEWTON-JOHN

★

"According to my parents," says Olivia New-ton-John, "as a kid I always sang, but strangely I sang harmonies rather than melody. My father always had classical music on—loud. Today classical music makes me sad. Big orchestras make me emotional."

The daughter of a college professor, Olivia was born in 1949 in Cambridge, England. Her father taught German at Kings College. Her grandfather, a Nobel prize-winning physicist, was Einstein's best friend. From these unusual academic roots has come a pop star. While growing up, she listened to pop records—Tennessee Ernie Ford, Ray Charles, Joan Baez, and Nina Simone.

When she was 5 her family moved to Australia. She grew up as a teenager in that country, which takes pride in her success. She still speaks with an Australian-British accent. At 11, her father and mother separated. At 13, her mother gave her an acoustic guitar. In her teen years, Olivia was shy. "I was 14 when I began going to dances on the University High grounds, and it was very traumatic. I was too scared to move." Later on, she conquered her shyness somewhat and joined a girls' group, the Sol Four, that sang in coffee houses. This led to appearances on Australian TV. Her first break came on a TV show, the *Kevin Dennis Auditions*, an amateur program. Then she won a talent contest; first prize was a trip to London. There she stayed, and made her way in pop music, eventually becoming quite popular in Britain before coming to the U.S.

In 1973 she received her first Grammy as "Best Female Country Vocalist" for her recording "Let Me Be There." In 1974 she won two more Grammys for "Record of the Year" and "Best Pop Vocal Performance," for "I Honestly Love You." In 1975 she was named "Top Female Vocalist" by *Billboard* and *Cashbox*.

5'4" Olivia has a sweet-sounding voice. Recently, she's tried to change her sound and her image from sweet girl to sexy lady. The part in *Grease* helped her make the transition. In 1979 she followed this up with a best-selling album, *Totally Hot*, which accented harder rock songs and arrangements.

She lives on a posh 4½ acre ranch near Malibu, not far from the Pacific Ocean. She rides horses and keeps cats (quite a few). She still carries on an Australian connection. Her record producer is Australian John Farrar. Olivia met him when he was a member of a pop group on a music show over there called *The Go Show*. He also writes songs tailor-made for Olivia. Her future in films look very good. Olivia hopes to do straight drama features as well as musicals. She treasures her film reviews of *Grease*, including one from *The New York Times*. In the part of Sandy, wrote the *Times*, "Olivia Newton-John, the recording star, was simultaneously funny and charming."

Among Olivia's LP's on MCA Records: *If You Love Me, Let Me Know, Have You Never Been Mellow, Clearly Love, Come on Over, Makin' a Good Thing Better*, and *Greatest Hits*.

DONNY AND
MARIE OSMOND

★

They sing, dance, do comedy and ice-skating routines, cut records, and appear in the movies and TV commercials. They're all-around entertainers, the biggest brother and sister act in show business. On TV they've done a lot of blue-eyed, black soul plus disco, along with middle-of-the-road Broadway and Hollywood "standards." On record, they stick pretty much to current pop sounds.

Donny (his full name is Donald Clark) plays a variety of instruments and sings. Marie sings and looks cute. She also does pretty well in comedy sketches. Both are practicing Mormons. In 1978 Donny got married to a 19-year-old Mormon girl, Debra Glenn. They live and do most of their work far from the tinseled factories of Hollywood in a $3 million show-biz complex in Utah, near Provo.

Cleancut types, Donny and Marie are good-looking in a toothpaste ad kind of way. Pop stars are supposed to be full of dope, surrounded by sex-mad groupies. They're supposed to break up hotel and motel rooms. Donny and Marie don't fit that mold. Somehow they manage to put over a modern, with-it appearance and yet hold on to conservative audiences. They follow Mormonism, which is a pretty strict moral code of conduct toward alcohol, pre-marital sex, and promiscuity. "The standards aren't hard to follow when you believe," says Donny.

Donny started to perform with his brothers, The Osmonds. He is fond of rhythm and blues. A gifted musician, he plays saxophone, piano, and organ. His mother taught him to play the saxophone. How did he start singing? "My brothers led the way. They sang as a quartet before I was interested. My first public performance was in Chicago when I was five years old."

Marie got into the family act early. When she was only four years old, she appeared on *The Andy Williams Show*, along with her brothers, then regulars on the TV program. She danced with the star. At nine, Marie joined the Osmonds as a key member. At 13, on her own, Marie had a major smash single, a country-flavored tune, "Paper Roses."

For several years, they had their own show on ABC-TV, *The Donny and Marie Show*. After a successful run of several years it was cancelled. Early in '79 they began hosting TV specials. One was an elaborate program shot in England, combining on-location shots of famed British landmarks as well as a filmed "live" concert. The other Osmond brothers still perform, sometimes with

Donny and Marie, and sometimes alone. They also act as executive producers of Donny and Marie TV shows.

Rock critics poke fun at the Donny and Marie brand of musicmaking. But Donny and his sister still manage to sell a lot of records on Polydor. Recent LPs: *Songs from the TV Show*, *Winning Combination*, *New Season*.

DOLLY PARTON

She wears platinum-colored hairdos as tall as a condominium. And her figure is on the plump, full, bosomy side. Yet Dolly doesn't mind too much what people say about her hair or looks. "Let 'em go," she says, "as long as they're talking about me." A practical, hard-working singer-songwriter, she's one of the top RCA country stars. Most of the year she tours, making personal appearances and giving concerts. She has already been cast in a major motion picture, *Nine to Five*, with Lily Tomlin and Jane Fonda.

She comes from a big, poor family—12 children—and was raised in the foothills of the Smoky Mountains of Tennessee. She started singing at seven, at home and in church. At 10 she sang on the radio. Besides singing she also writes songs.

The day after she graduated high school, Dolly decided to go for broke. She came to Nashville with a cardboard suitcase packed with her music and lyrics. She went around peddling them to record producers and performers. Sometimes she sang them, and accompanied herself on guitar. Sometimes she'd show up with demos she cut herself, demonstrating her tunes and making contacts. Her first contract was with a local country label, Monument.

Dolly plays acoustic guitar and banjo. At one point she tried teaching herself the electric guitar. Pop writers describe her voice as "small but sweet"; others say it is a childlike soprano. In 1978 she was chosen by *Billboard* as the year's number-one female country music artist. She was also named the number-one female album artist in the country music field for her single record, "Here You Come Again." Put into an album of the same title, the LP became the first platinum record by a female country singer.

She's sympathetic to women who are strong and practical. On stage she is quite a sight with tight white pants, jewelry and sequins, and her towering hairdo. She's five feet tall, wears five-inch heels and heavy make-up. Country music fans love her. "They can detect a sincerity and honesty in what I'm singing to them," she says.

The lady of a hundred wigs has also got a brain. She writes a lot of her songs "on the road" in a bus. Some describe her songs as "slices of life." Using the country idiom, she comments on life, the bumpy road to romance, and unwed mothers. Many other singers, including Linda Ronstadt, Emmylou Harris, and Maria Muldaur record Dolly Parton songs. Along with songs, Dolly jots down thoughts, children's stories, and novels, which so far have been unpublished. She enjoys writing,

"I want to be known as a great writer. That's a dream of mine," she says.

Her husband, Carl Dean, is in the asphalt business. They live in Tara, a 100-acre, 23-room mansion outside of Nashville, In '79 she also took "a city place" in New York, a fancy office-apartment overlooking Fifth Avenue and Central Park. Cool and chic, it's decorated with modern non-objective art as well as scenes of Tennessee. "I'm a happy person," she says, "because I don't like trouble."

Dolly on LP: *Heartbreaker, Here You Come Again, New Harvest—First Gathering, Coat of Many Colors*.

TEDDY PENDERGRASS

In many places music is being cut out of school programs, and with it, music enrichment, bands, and glee clubs. Budget cutbacks. Luckily, when Teddy Pendergrass went to school there were music programs. In Philadelphia, Pennsylvania, where he grew up, he sang with the city-wide McIntyre Elementary School Choir and later, with the All-City Stetson Junior High School Choir. Of course, singing in a school glee club didn't make him a pop star; the singing, the material is different. But it didn't hurt.

Throughtout the years, women have swooned and swayed to the music and sight of "heartthrobs" like Frank Sinatra, Elvis Presley, and Mick Jagger. Teddy Pendergrass is a black romantic figure. *Variety* calls him "the sex symbol of soul." One of his gimmicks at concerts (sometimes advertised as "For Women Only") is to kiss girls sitting up front. He's even done this at the prestigious Avery Fisher Hall in New York's Lincoln Center.

Of his album, *Life Is a Song Worth Singing*, Robert Christgrau of the *Village Voice* wrote, "Romantic shlock at its sexiest and most honest." He gave it a rating of A Minus. Musically, Teddy has a soft, slightly raspy voice. He can belt too. Mostly, he accents slower soul songs and songs he did when he was connected with Harold Melvin and the Blue Notes.

If you believe his bio, Teddy started singing at two, was an "ordained minister" at 10, and a self-taught drummer at 13. Probably his most formal musical training came when he sang in the school glee clubs. As teenager, Teddy joined a local Philadelphia pop group and became its lead singer. He decided not to pursue singing as career when he was "taken" by an "I'll make you a star" slickster. That man, claiming to be singer James Brown's brother, promised him a spectacular career. It never happened.

Disillusioned, Teddy turned to performing as a drummer with another local singing group, the Cadillacs. It was as a drummer that Teddy first met Harold Melvin, lead singer with the Blue Notes. Having lost their backup band, the Blue Notes recruited the Cadillacs and with them came drummer Teddy Pendergrass.

In 1970, during a tour of the French West Indies, Teddy got a chance to sing. Some members of Blue Notes cut out and several new people joined the vocal/instrumental band. Teddy was asked to step in as lead singer with the newly reconstructed Blue Notes.

In 1971 the band signed with Philadelphia International Records, which was run by two record producer-songwriters, Keny Gawlee and Leon Huff. Their first release for the label, *I Miss You*, officially introduced Teddy Pendergrass to the record-buying public. Response to the record was very good as were the reviews. With Pendergrass as lead singer, a string of Blue Notes hits followed: "If You Don't Know Me By Now" (1972), "The Love I Lost" (1973), "To Be True" (1975), and "Bad Luck" (1975)—all certified gold. Then came the release of a new Blue Notes album, *Wake Up Everybody*. The LP was to be Teddy's farewell recording with the Blue Notes.

Following the widely publicized Blue Notes split-up in 1976, Pendergrass re-signed with Philadelphia International Records. His first solo effort, *Teddy Pendergrass*, was released in 1977. It was a huge success and included the singles "I Don't Love You Anymore," "You Can't Hide From Yourself," and "The More I Get the More I Want," all of which were disco hits as well.

THE RAMONES

There's a new wave of hard rockers, the post-Rolling Stones generation. A leader of the pack is a New York band, The Ramones. They offer high voltage "punk rock." Its members are young men from Forest Hills, N.Y., a comfortable middle-class neighborhood of brown-bricked Tudor homes, one family wooden frame houses, and giant apartment houses. Mostly their sounds are shattering, but their material has a point of view, that of the rootless, angry adolescents you often see hanging around pizza parlors.

The Ramones are loud, but they also have a sense of deadpan comedy. Generally, their song titles are aggressive, catchy, and negative: "I Wanna Be Sedated," "Loudmouth," and "Cretin Hop." Occasionally they weaken and do a ballad ("Needles and Pins," an oldie).

The *Village Voice* rock critics love them. Robert Christgrau calls them a "great group," and gave their fourth album, *Road to Ruin* (Sire Records), a rating of A. In an article in *Trouser Press* there

is applause for a Ramones' song, "I Just Want Something to Do." This is supposed to be a new anthem for bored and frustrated teenagers who can't find a place in society.

On stage, they look wild, geeky. As Johnny Ramone once said, "When we play videotapes of ourselves, we look like a bunch of freaks." The present lineup of the Ramones are: Joey Ramone (vocals), Johnny Ramone (guitar), Dee Dee Ramone (bass) and Marky Ramone (drums). They signed with Sire in 1976.

Lead singer Joey Ramone is often called a copyist. One rock critic referring to *Road to Ruin* wrote, "Over the last two years, he has stolen just about every effect of the early British rock singers." But increasingly he is being himself musically.

The official bio of the group in a typical sample of hype says: "When their debut album, *Ramones*, was released in April 1976, it jolted music critics and record buyers around the world out of their pseudo-progressive music doldrums and into a whole new level of rock and roll consciousness. The reaction was so strong that *Ramones* is still uncontested as the most talked about, written about, and most controversial album of 1976."

Their second LP was *Leave Home*. Captivated by their first album, more than 200 members of the rock press of New York crammed into a tiny studio to hear it. Reviews of it that followed were good, and soon pictures of the Ramones started to appear in pop/rock magazines. They were on their way and soon they were getting concert bookings. Other rock figures and groups came to listen too.

In mid 1977 the Ramones released their third album, *Rocket To Russia*. It soon became clear that the band, originally thought of as a "one-shot wonder," was here to stay. The Ramones became the first new wave band to break the top 100 with their single "Sheena Is A Punk Rocker" and in early 1978 went even higher in the charts with "Rockaway Beach."

In front of packed houses throughout Europe and America, the Ramones have brought audiences to their feet screaming for encores.

On Sire: *The Road to Ruin*.

LOU RAWLS

Not a hard rocker, Lou Rawls has been able to keep on top with his warm singing style and his bright personality. 1978 was a very good year for Lou. He was the Budweiser song-spokesman on TV. He appeared on TV a lot, including *The Muppet Show*. He was a "star presenter" at the 21st Grammy Awards. Also, he loomed large in the record business with a "live" album recorded from the stage of the Mark Hellinger Theatre on Broadway, where he starred in a one-man show.

Called "The Natural Man" after a hit record of his, Rawls is part of a pop vocal tradition that's pre-rock: that of Nat King Cole, Perry Como, Billy Eckstine, Dick Haymes, and Frank Sinatra. It's a soft ballad-swing tradition. "His voice comes from the same kind of deep resonant source as Nat [King] Cole's," wrote John Wilson of *The New York Times*. He also does Louis Armstrong jazz classics with warmth, humor, and that Armstrong deep-down growl.

Rawls is from the South Side of Chicago, born

Dec. 1, 1936. At seven he was singing with the junior choir of the Greater Mount Olive Baptist Church. As a teenager he formed a pop singing group. In those days the vocal models were such black singers as Curtis Mayfield, The Flamingos, The Staple Singers, and Nat King Cole. After a stint in the Army as a paratrooper, where he made 32 jumps, he joined a group called The Pilgrim Travelers. While traveling, there was a bad traffic accident and Lou almost died. In 1960 he was discovered. During the sixties he was a smash as a solo artist and one of the biggest stars on Capitol Records. "The King" (Nat Cole), who was Lou's idol, also recorded for that company.

Lou sang of love, but also of poverty ("Dead End Street"), and the good times. He won Grammys in 1967 for "Dead End Street" and in 1971 for "Natural Man." However, in the mid-seventies, with rock and country holding forth, Lou's recording career dipped. It was a frustrating, painful time. Along came two of the most successful of the "now" producers, Kenny Gamble and Leon Huff of Philadelphia International Records. They thought that Lou could still make it on disc. And he has.

In 1976 he hit the charts with a ballad, "You'll Never Find Another Love Like Mine." And since signing with Philadelphia International, which distributes via Columbia, he has also recorded one platinum album (*All Things In Time*) and two gold albums (*Unmistakably Lou* in 1977 and *When You've Heard Lou You've Heard It All* in 1978).

Through the years Lou Rawls has also assisted black kids to get started in show business.

HELEN REDDY

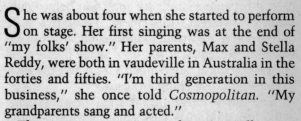

S he was about four when she started to perform
on stage. Her first singing was at the end of
"my folks' show." Her parents, Max and Stella
Reddy, were both in vaudeville in Australia in the
forties and fifties. "I'm third generation in this
business," she once told *Cosmopolitan*. "My
grandparents sang and acted."

The singer-songwriter was born in Melbourne,
Australia, Oct. 25, 1942. As a child she worked
with her parents in and around Australia, sometimes singing, sometimes acting in comedy
sketches. "I grew up immersed in show business,
studied piano for years, guitar, voice, dance. I
hoofed in the chorus line for ages. I even fiddled
on the bass violin, and I had a classical training
in Shakespeare."

This marvelous training led to her having her
own TV show in Australia, *Helen Reddy Sings*.
However, she felt that she was boxed in in her
native land. So she departed for New York. In 1968
she went to a party and met a high-powered ex-

agent, former college history major, Jeff Wald. He fought to push her career. One of her first jobs was at an Irish bar in New York City in which she sang all night for $50. Jeff approached most of the record companies with demos of Helen, but they thought her voice wasn't "commercial."

Her big break came in 1971, when after much nagging, Capitol recorded Helen singing, "I Don't Know How to Love Him" from *Jesus Christ Superstar*. That did pretty well, but she hit it big with a song she herself wrote, "I Am Woman." Jeff didn't like it, but Helen did. She cut it in 1972 and it proved to be a fabulous smash. More than that, it became a landmark song that helped publicize the women's movement. The lyrics state that women are strong, courageous, and can do anything. Recently, it was used as the theme song for the International Women's Year and the ERA (Equal Rights Amendment) cause.

Her voice is easygoing, straight-ahead without frills. Her diction is clear. She reportedly earns more than $3 million a year from records, concerts, TV, and performance monies as a composer-lyricist. She has appeared as a permanent host on TV's *Midnight Special*, and is scheduled to be in a series of prime-time specials.

She and her family live in an estate in Brentwood, California, with swimming pool and tennis court. Besides her career, she raises money for causes of interest to her (ecology, women's rights) and for politicians she favors (Governor Jerry Brown). She has two children, Traci, 15, and Jordan, 6, and two dogs. Her first movie was a Walt Disney musical, *Pete's Dragon*.

Helen on gold-album LPs include: *Love Song for Jeffrey, Free and Easy, No Way to Treat a Lady, Helen Reddy's Hits, I Don't Know How to Love Him, Music Music.* Platinum albums: *I Am Woman, Long Hard Climb, Helen Reddy's Greatest Hits.*

KENNY ROGERS

Once he was the leader of a pop group with a soft rockin', gentle sound called Kenny Rogers and The First Edition. It made quite a splash, but since then he has gone solo, recording for United Artists Records. He has moved away from the folk/rock to embrace Nashville, but with the same gentle approach.

In a review of Rogers' nightclub act in Las Vegas, *Variety* wrote: "Little has changed around the basic Rogers. He sold his songs back then with low-key persuasion, marked by some vocal gimmickry, including a pulsating vibrato and glottal growl."

He wears his hair longish, with a part down the middle. It's black with strong patches of gray and white. His beard has the pepper-and-salt look too. Not long ago he picked up two big honors at the 1979 American Music Awards for favorite country male vocalist and best country album *(Ten Years of Gold)*.

Born in 1941, he's a native of Houston, Texas.

Kenny left that city with a regional hit, "Crazy Feeling," determined to pursue a career in the music business. What followed was a stretch as a member of the Bobby Doyle Trio. In 1966 he moved onto join the New Christy Minstrels. A year later Kenny, Mike Settle, Terry Williams, and Thelma Camacho left the Minstrels to form The First Edition — a rock band typical of the psychedelic sixties. The group pushed on to national stature on the heels of hits like "Just Dropped in to See What Condition My Condition Was In," "But You Know I Love You," "Ruby (Don't Take Your Love to Town)," "Tell It All, Brother," "Heed the Call," "Ruben James," and "Something's Burnin'."

The band moved progressively away from the hard, acid-tinged rock of the time and closer to the more mellow country sound with each successive release. When the group finally disbanded and Kenny set out on his own, the progression toward country music was complete. He signed with United Artists Records and Nashville producer Larry Butler. The new combination proved to be fruitful as the two scored quickly with "Love Lifted Me," "Homemade Love," Laura," and "While the Feeling's Good." Then came Kenny's version of "Lucille," which propelled him to superstardom. A Grammy, a prestigious list of awards, and invitations to host *The Tonight Show* followed, enlarging Kenny's rapidly building following.

Kenny is a compulsive worker, touring most of the year. When not on the road or in the studio he can be found in his Los Angeles home with wife, Marianne Gordon, a regular on the popular syndicated television series *Hee Haw*. Their home, by the way, includes a 50' x 20' fish pond, stocked with some 115 Koi carp. Kenny is also an active athlete. He's considered a first-rate competitive tennis player and an accomplished softball pitcher. He has sponsored a celebrity tennis match for charity in San Diego and each year he stages a celebrity softball game in Las Vegas for the benefit of the Nevada Special Olympics for the mentally retarded.

On LP: *Kenny Rogers, Every Time Two Fools Collide, The Gambler, Daytime Friends.*

★
THE
ROLLING STONES
★

Controversial, the Rolling Stones continue to be known as the bad boys of rock, even though they are approaching their forties. They've been linked to decadence, drugs, riotous road tours, and general hell-raising. Musically, they have been described as a "grinding, tingling band." The voicings are harsh, rarely tender or warm, a sort of leather-jacket sound. The British pop group has its roots in American black rhythm and blues, although the blues are far more sensitive, compassionate, even humorous.

Some consider them the oldest and best rock band in existence. In 1978 they hit the top of the charts with a new LP, *Some Girls*. In that same year, they toured the U.S., and in seven weeks, grossed more than nine million dollars. For the record, the Stones have cut 17 albums for London Records, eight for Atlantic, so far, plus another

LP, *Metamorphosis*, released by Allen Klein. When you stop to think of it, wrote the *New York Post*, "it is amazing that this band has remained on top, year after year, for 16 years."

One reason they are controversial is their songs, which use plain language and say things that bother people. "I Can't Get No Satisfaction" is a harsh cry of frustration. "Mother's Little Helper" jabs at mothers who take alcohol and pills and then try to tell young people how to live. Another Stones' favorite is "Let's Spend the Night Together." That one, seeming to suggest sexual permissiveness, caused an uproar in Britain and the U.S. "Under My Thumb," states that girls ought to toe the line, which makes women's lib unhappy. The use of drugs has also been popularized by the Stones in their own personal life-style, and in such songs as "Sister Morphine."

Recently, Reverend Jesse Jackson, U.S. civil rights leader, attacked the title song of the Rolling Stones' *Some Girls* LP as racist slur on black women. Mick Jagger and Keith Richards are the songwriters of the group. Mostly, Mick writes the music, Keith the lyrics. But two of the strong songs associated with the Stones are by Mick Jagger (words and music), "Gimme Shelter" and "Street Fighting Man." "Street Fighting Man" is vaguely political but says, "what can a poor boy do except to sing for a rock and roll band?"

In terms of image, they've gone on to fame, portraying a kind of working-class discontent. Kids turned to The Stones rather than to Karl Marx. The Rolling Stones have taken pot shots at the establishment, motherhood, manners. With this attitude they have all become pop millionaires. *The Superstars of Rock*, a book published in England, says, "The Stones' scowl became as tantalizing as the Beatles grin."

The band is led by a powerful on-stage performer Michael "Mick" Jagger, who was born July 26, 1944, in Kent, England. Black-eyed, brown-haired, 5'10" Mick is the son of a physical education teacher, Joseph Jagger, and his wife Eva. Mick, who's considered well-read, attended the famed London School of Economics. He himself taught physical education and sports on a U.S. Army base. He's had no musical education, but began singing with a blues group in 1961. Now separated from his wife, Bianca, he has a seven-year-old daughter, Jade.

In 1962, Mick, Brian Jones, Keith Richards, Bill Wyman, Charlie Watts, and Ian Stewart started playing together. In June 1963 they produced their first single record, "Come On." Their first LP, *The Rolling Stones*, appeared in April 1964. Along the way, Stewart dropped out. Mick Taylor came on board ('69–'74), and so did Ron Wood, Billy Preston, and Ollie Brown for varying periods. On June 3, 1969, Brian died from a drug overdose in a house once owned by A.A. Milne, author of *Winnie the Pooh*.

The Rolling Stones have been seen in practically every documentary about the history of rock. Mick himself has acted in two films: *Performance*, in which he played a wealthy rock star; and *Ned Kelley*, the story of an Australian outlaw folk hero.

Rolling Stones singles: "Let's Spend the Night Together," "Get Off My Cloud," "Honky Tonk

Women," "Paint It Black," "It's Only Rock and Roll," "Let It Bleed." Their LPs include: *The Rolling Stones First Album, Out of Our Heads, Get Yer Ya-Yas Out, Big Hits, Through the Past Darkly, Sticky Fingers, It's Only Rock and Roll, Live, Some Girls,* and *Love You.*

LINDA RONSTADT

Linda Ronstadt was a lonely, sad child who felt overshadowed by her brother and older sister. Today she is one of the most successful female rock stars in the world and is still singing about loneliness and the need to feel loved. Her German mother and her German-Mexican father ran a hardware stone in Tucson, Arizona. Her father sang and played guitar, and her mother played banjo. At age four Linda was singing harmony with them.

After one semester at Arizona State University she went to L.A., where she met Kenny Edwards and Bob Kimmel and formed the Stone Poneys. They made three albums and had one hit single, "Different Drum." They broke up in 1967. Linda made her first solo album in 1969, *Home Sown, Home Grown,* and her second LP, *Silk Purse,* led to her first solo hit record, "Long Long Time." But she had to wait four years for another hit and kept hunting for a sound she wanted — a blend of pop and country music.

In 1974 Linda and producer-manager Peter Asher formed a partnership and their first album, *Heart Like a Wheel*, made her a star.

Has success brought happiness? Not exactly. One of her saddest songs, "Desperado," concerns a person who only wants "the things that you can't get." She says the song is about herself. Most often her songs are defiant, or bittersweet and always unsettling. But *The New York Times* music critic, John Rockwell says, "Even when she's professing weakness her voice is so strong you never quite believe it." She has said of her success: "I get kicked in the teeth as well as rewarded for success. In the whole world there is no free lunch."

Linda spends several months a year looking for new album material and recording it. The rest of the time she is on the road, singing. She travels with an all-male band, a female secretary, and a makeup artist. She has been known to play poker with "the boys." Keeping her weight down is a constant battle and recently she ate so little she developed a vitamin deficiency which resulted in her legs turning black and blue.

Linda has said, "The price I pay for my life-style is not being able to have domesticity." She also said, "Domestic bliss must be the highest form of bliss a human being can experience. I have profound respect for it. A woman who can do all it involves and have a career is really the exception."

Her name has been linked with Mick Jagger, comedian Bill Murray, and Chip Carter (son of the President), but the most visible romance she has had is with Governor Jerry Brown of California. About eight years ago in Lucy Casada's El Adobe

Café, each of them sat in separate booths enjoying enchiladas. The proprietor, Frank Casada, encouraged his wife to introduce them and the friendship blossomed. Both love ethnic chow, funky music, and privacy. An old aide of Brown's says, "It's a very special relationship they have. It's a very important thing and it's not something either of them takes lightly." When they began dating, Linda subscribed to the *Wall Street Journal* and *The New York Times* so she could hold up her end of the conversation. Friends say Brown has said he couldn't marry Linda because it would cost him the White House. Linda was said to react to that by swearing to wear basic black and pearls for life if he would change his mind. Last year their trip to Africa was covered widely in newspapers and magazines and some felt it didn't do Brown's career any good. However, on February 17, 1980, Linda did her bit for Jerry's campaign by appearing with a group of rollerskating celebrities at L.A.'s *Flippers*, to raise funds for Brown's presidential bid.

Linda is the only female performer to have five consecutive platinum albums, *(Heart Like a Wheel, Prisoner in Disguise, Hasten Down the Wind, Simple Dreams,* and *Living in the USA).* Her *Greatest Hits* album also went platinum. *Mad Love* is the title of her newest 1980 album release.

DIANA ROSS

A divorced mother of three, Ms. Ross continues to be one of the most glamorous figures in pop. *People* magazine once described her as "Glitter Chic incarnate, a flash of furs and facets and long cars." Friends know her for her hawklike devotion to her children, Rhonda, 8, Tracee, 7, and Chudney, 4. The public knows her mostly as the former member of the Supremes, who split away from that group at the height of its popularity and went on to carve out a fabulous career of her own as a solo recording artist, concert headliner, and film star. Since those early days, Diana has recorded more than 18 solo albums on Motown, many of them gold records.

She's come a long way from the Brewster Homes, a Detroit housing project. Up to recently, she lived in a 12-room Beverly Hills mansion in California. Now she lives in the Big Apple, in a posh, 31st-floor apartment in New York's Sherry Netherland Hotel. She says her kids are her "first priority," but she doesn't neglect business either.

She's a disciplined, hard worker.

Diana has a smallish voice that she uses effectively. She can do soft pop/soul-type songs that come out of Motown's dream factory, as well as Broadway ballads and funky street material. She can be kittenish and earthy. Diana can also do comedy, and has done good imitations of Harpo Marx and Charles Chaplin on TV.

Strong-willed she can be cold too. "I've been cold. I've been uptight," she admitted in an interview with Barbara Walters of ABC, "but I've gotten better."

Born Mar. 26, 1945, as a teen-ager she was part of a trio called The Primettes, along with Mary Wilson and Florence Ballard. The trio sang around Detroit — in schools and churches — determined to be known in the world of music. Naturally, the trio gravitated to Detroit's Motown Records. Renamed the Supremes, the rest is a chunk of musical history. Las Vegas, New York, television, worldwide tours, the Supremes were just that — supreme. Then after agonizing over the decision, Diana left the group in 1969 to pursue a solo career.

Early in 1976 Diana Ross made a triumphant tour of Europe, followed by her Broadway debut at the Palace Theatre which broke the all-time 63-year-old house record. For this she got a Tony Award. Next came an NBC *Big Event Special,* the first 90-minute one-woman prime-time special on TV.

Motown president, Berry Gordy, Jr., who has guided her career from the beginning, helped put her in the movies. He put his savings on the line to finance Diana's first film, *Lady Sings The Blues,* a biography of the late jazz singer, Billie Holiday. While she couldn't match Billie's style, she did such a very good acting job that she was nominated for an Academy Award for Best Actress. Her other films include *Mahogany* and the super-expensive *The Wiz*.

Her LPs include: *Diana Ross, An Evening with Diana Ross,* and *Diana Ross' Greatest Hits.* And if you want to check out the early Diana as part of the Supremes, some of those LPs are still in catalogue and "golden oldie" record shops.

Number-one single records include: "Reach Out and Touch (Somebody's Hand)" and "Ain't No Mountain High Enough."

SANTANA

There's a lot of Latin-American influence in today's pop. Hit songs ("Girl from Ipanema") and catchy rhythmic patterns and dances (samba, cha-cha, salsa) have worked their way to America and into American pop. Among the talents that excel in it are: Tito Puente, Willie Bobo, Pacheco, Sergio Mendes, and Antonio Jobim. Another big name is a Chicano bandleader-songwriter, Carlos Santana. His brand of music is Latin rock, mixing jazz, rhythm and blues, and Latin soul.

"It is the duty of the musician," says Carlos Santana, "to bring joy." In his band he is the lead singer and lead guitarist. Born in Autlan de Navarro, Mexico, he started playing the violin at the age of five. Later he took up the guitar because he was playing too many notes on the violin. At 14, Carlos was playing in assorted sleazy bars in Tijuana. Then he moved to San Francisco, where he first created a splash on the stage of Fillmore West. Then his group was known as the Santana Blues Band.

However, he didn't receive a record offer till he made a striking appearance at the Woodstock Festival in 1969. That same year Columbia signed him and his first LP, *Santana,* broke out and sold two million copies. Since then he has made many records, and performed all over the world. His first albums were raw and gritty. Later he turned to more complicated, experimental, intellectual kinds of music as he tried to incorporate spiritual feelings derived from a guru, Sri Chinmoy (*Caravamserai* and *Welcome*). In recent years he has returned to his barrio roots with such albums as *Amigos, Festival,* and *Moonflower.* In 1978 he had a Top-10 single hit called "Moonflower."

Santana rarely plays for dances, but not long ago he and Tito Puente had a silly "battle of the bands" at New York's Roseland. His band began with "Carnival," filled with much Brazilian street percussion before moving neatly into his current hit, "Let the Children Play," prompting five thousand pairs of hands to cut loose in *clave* (applause). Carlos was up there on stage, playing lead guitar, strutting and blowing a whistle.

Santana uses a lot of Latin-American instruments: bongos, congas, timbales, as well as more orthodox bass, guitar, drums, and keyboard. He's a bit of a philosopher. Not long ago he dedicated one of his LPs to Bob Dylan, Stevie Wonder, and Muhammed Ali because they are "incredible warriors on the battlefield of life."

On LP: *Abraxas, Festival, Inner Secrets, Moonflower.*

SEALS AND CROFTS

★

Texans are supposed to be loud and boastful. Jim Seals (born in Sidney, Texas) and Dash Crofts (Cisco, Texas) are natives of The Lone Star State but they're soft spoken and low-key. This Warner Bros. Records team has been making music for 20 years. They paid their dues with lots of road touring. One group they toured with all over North America and Asia was the Champs. "Being on the road with the Champs was like being in the Army," says Dash Crofts. "Someone told you when to get up, how to dress, where to go, what to play, and how to play it."

Since they have carved out their niche in the world of pop, they enjoy a more laid-back life-style out in California. They work in the sleepy little community of San Fernando. They love it because it's far from the neon glitter of Hollywood rock and roll.

There they live with family and children, making music and practicing a relaxed way of life, guided by the teaching of Baha'i. When they want to record, they walk down the road to Dawnbreeker Studios, their own 32-track facility in a sprawling adobe house that also houses the comfortable offices of their management agency and publishing companies.

Musically, they are known for their intricate, subtle vocal harmonies. Jim Seals plays acoustic guitar and fiddle; Dash plays piano, drums, and electric mandolin. They do bluegrass, country music, soul, rock. Lately, they've been adding a touch of Middle-Eastern sound. In 1978 in their eleventh LP for Warner Bros., *Takin' It Easy*, they introduced the santour, a Persian instrument virtually unknown in the U.S. (Persia is now Iran.)

Jim Seals started playing the fiddle and picking out chords on his father's guitar when he was five. Later he turned to tenor sax, and by his early teens had filled a three-ring notebook with original songs. Dash Crofts was playing piano at the age of four, and by seven had learned to play drums as well.

Seals and Crofts met during their teens in a Texas junior high school and there formed their first group. They jammed together throughout high school. In 1958 Jim and Dash headed for California. At first they worked as studio musicians in Los Angeles, doing gigs for such performers as Glen Campbell, Sonny & Cher, The Monkees, and Lenny Welch. With the Champs they recorded a rock standard, "Tequilla" which sold more than six million copies on Challenge Records. That band toured internationally for seven years before breaking up.

Seals and Crofts manage to work at their own speed, surrounded by an extended family of wives, children, and friends. They guest-star on TV shows, and for relaxation play in various golf tournaments. Their LPs include: *Year of Sunday*, *Summer Breeze*, *Diamond Girl*, *Unborn Child*, *I'll Play for You*, *Seals and Crofts' Greatest Hits*, *Get Closer*, *Sudan Village*, and *One on One* (soundtrack album for an animated film).

NEIL SEDAKA

His daughter Dara started to record at the age of 14. That's about the time Neil Sedaka himself started to listen to popular music and pick out tunes on the piano. His parents were trained pianists and his grandmother studied with Walter Damrosch, who used to teach music appreciation to young people (the classics) over the radio in New York. So music was in the air at the Sedaka home in Brooklyn, New York.

The singer-pianist-composer was born Mar.13, 1939. He is a keen student of the pop music charts and generally the things he writes follows what's selling. Most of his songs are teenage fluff such as "Oh, Carole." However, once in a while he cuts loose with a few tunes of greater melodic and rhythmic strength. These include "Love Will Keep Us Together" (a contemporary standard) and "Strolling in the Country After the Rain."

On stage, Neil is a pleasant, amiable performer. Mostly he sings at the piano. Sometimes he goes stage center to sing and do a few elementary movements. Sedaka is chunky and boyish-faced, and lives in New York City. A wealthy pop figure, he recently told TV's Dick Clark that he has written "over 1,000 songs." He is very popular in Japan. His wife aids him on the business side.

When he graduated from high school, he haunted Tin Pan Alley, and along with a high school friend, lyricist Howard Greenfield, formed a team. They eventually tied up with a rock publishing company, Kirshner and Nevins (Kirshner now hosts a popular synidicated TV show). For that firm Neil became a contract writer for a weekly salary. A demo on which he sang one of his songs caught the ear of Steve Sholes (Sholes was the man who brought Elvis Presley to RCA). That's how Sedaka became a recording artist on RCA. Quickly Sedaka recorded several hit singles including, "The Diary," "No Vacancy," and "I Go Ape."

In the two years that followed, Sedaka became a top performer in the world of soft, easygoing rock. He gave concerts, and showed up on TV shows such as Dick Clark's *American Bandstand* and *The Ed Sullivan Show*. He also continued writing hits. But somehow, by early 1962, his fame fizzled out. He dropped performing but continued to write.

In the mid-sixties Sedaka and Greenfield proceeded to write many hits for other groups and artists. He co-authored "Working on a Groovy Thing," recorded by the Fifth Dimension, and "Rainy Jane," cut by Davy Jones of the Monkees, and many others. Today the Sedaka catalogue is very valuable and includes a vintage favorite, "Breaking Up Is Hard to Do."

In the early seventies he picked up his recording career once again on Kirshner Records. Now he records for Elektra/Asylum, which is part of the giant Warner Bros. conglomerate. Neil on LP: *Many Sides, All You Need, A Song.*

★

BOB SEGER

★

A working-class type, his teen years were spent in Ann Arbor, Michigan, fooling around in cars, à la the film, *American Graffiti*. His father worked as a medic for the Ford Motor Co. and played clarinet with a 13-piece band. Things were okay until his father ran away. The Seger family then suffered proverty. Bob shared one room with his brother George, a bed, and a hot plate. His music idol in his teen years was Del Shannon, a Midwest pop favorite whose big hit was "Runaway."

At 15 Seger made his debut as a singer on a cheap acetate demo disk. He had written the song too. That gave him a direction. In 1961 he joined a three-piece band called the Detibels. It played high school talent shows and University of Michigan fraternity parties. Later he worked with other rock bands in clubs and cheap honky tonk bars. Of his teen years Seger says, "I had slicked down hair like a greaser, and dressed in Banlons and pegged pants. A typical hoodlum in a dark jacket."

In the mid-sixties, Seger started to come up with his brand of straight-ahead, no-frills rock and roll.

Crawdaddy describes him as "leading man to a hungry generation stranded in alienating jobs in auto plants." He slowly built up a fanatical hometown following around Detroit and the Midwest, but it wasn't easy. A lot of things got him down. "The road, the loneliness in your hotel room and making records — it's a lonesome, frustrating process."

In 1969 he cut his first hit, "Ramblin' Gamblin' Man." His next biggie was "Beautiful Loser" in 1976. Next came the blockbuster that really put him over, an LP called *Night Moves,* which has sold more than two million copies on Capitol.

He looks like a rocker, with flowing brown hair. On stage he flashes powerhouse energy. Off stage he relaxes in a modest ranch house about 50 miles from Detroit. He has a lakefront cabin which has a 36 ft. Chris Craft. His backup group is called the Silver Bullet Band. He's cut down on his personal appearances but he still does more than 100 personal appearances a year to keep his name shiny and to promote his records.

Seger's early days of poverty haunt him. And it's why he won't record anybody else's songs but his own. He's worked 15 years to reach the position, and he's not giving anything away. One of his songs from *Stranger in Town* is a sort of protest song.

> I feel like a number
> I'm not a number
> I'm not a number
> Damit, I'm a man
> I said I'm a man

© Bob Seger 1977 Gear Publishing Co.

★

SHA NA NA

★

There's a comic side of pop. You get bursts of humor in *Grease*, the LPs of Cheech and Chong, the clowning of Bette Midler, and the work of Sha Na Na. On records, on syndicated TV, and in concert, the 10-member group has won quite a following as they poke fun at the golden oldies, the sounds of the hit groups and stars of yesteryear.

They are a vocal and instrumental group that does movement and bits of choreography. They have a field day kidding vintage rockers, TV dance contests, the wearing of dark glasses, the hair-combing, and low-brow slang. According to an official bio, they helped inspire the musical, *Grease* (they appeared in the movie version). For that film, one member of Sha Na Na, Screamin' Scott, wrote "Sandy," one of the tunes sung by John Travolta.

The satirical group started out as an acapella choir (singing without instrumental backing) as students of Columbia University in 1969. They performed in a campus cafeteria called "The Lion's Den," singing contemporary tunes. Nothing. Then they rented some old gold lamé costumes, greased their hair, and sang a set of 1950s rock 'n' roll. Instant hit. Later, they wowed the campus with a show, "The Glory That Was Grease," then followed that with an outdoor performance, "Grease Under the Stars."

The response was so rewarding that they decided to quit giving it away and turn professional. They appropriately took their name from the background vocal of a song entitled "Get a Job." After a sucessful gig at Fillmore East they were dropped into the middle of Woodstock '69 as a change-of-pace group. Instant hit.

Following the Peace and Love festival, they toured the U.S., played Europe, and cut records. Along with personal appearances they were booked on TV — Johnny Carson, a John Lennon/Yoko special, and *Midnight Special*. In 1977 Sha Na Na began its own syndicated TV program which continued in '78 and '79.

Four of the pioneers of Sha Na Na still remain. They are Scott "Santini" Powell; Denny Greene, the black member of the group; Donny York, with his striped tank shirts and shades, from Boise, Idaho; and drummer John (Jocko) Marcellino. Additions: Lennie Baker known in Boston jazz circles as "Two-Ton Lennie"; Jon (Bowzer) Bauman, the 6'2", 150-pound stringbean with the deep voice and hawklike visage; John (Johnny) Contardo, vocalist with the deceptive choirboy looks; "Dirty Dan" McBride, the lead guitarist; bass guitarist David (Chico) Ryan; and "Screamin' Scott" Simon, the pianist with Jerry Lee Lewis style.

On LP: *The Golden Age of Rock 'n' Roll*, *Here to Bud*.

CARLY SIMON

She comes from a distinguished and talented family. Her father was co-founder of Simon & Schuster, the big publishing house. One of her cousins is George Simon, the authority on swing and the big bands and executive director of The National Academy of Recording Arts and Sciences. Carly is an attractive singer-songwriter. She's married to pop star James Taylor. The pop couple have a son and a daughter.

The attractive singer-songwriter was born in New York City, June 25, 1945. Her father played piano (Chopin, Bach). Her mother sang everything from lullabies to Gershwin. Her early interest was folk music. She attended Sarah Lawrence College and there, she and her sister, Lucy, performed at school functions as the Simon Sisters. Later the two of them performed at folk clubs in and around New York. When Lucy got married and quit the business Carly continued on her own.

Carly's first solo recording never came out; the tapes still lie in the Columbia Records vaults somewhere. In 1970 she signed with Elektra. In 1971 she came out with her first LP, a grab bag of rock, folk, ballads, country, and even bluegrass, titled *Carly Simon*. It went up into the charts. Since then she has been a significant figure on the pop scene. The Elektra Records star, after all these years, still has a fear of performing in public. Until lately she has refused to go on tour or perform in clubs to hype her record sales. She's got a strong homebody domestic streak.

There's a gutsy hipness and eye for satire in her lyrics ("You're So Vain"). Musically, she's a mix of folk and soft rock, with a touch of country. Her voice is an effective instrument; it doesn't have the other worldly quality of some women folk-singers.

Of her personality she says: "I'm not just one person, nor do I try to define myself. My image changes a lot according to how I feel physically, or my mood, or whether I'm angry about something. Some days you get up and think, 'Hey, I'm beautiful, and I'm going to sock it to 'em,' and other days you say, 'I feel fat and I'm going to wear something real loose and baggy and just be the nice girl next door.' "

Carly and her husband have two homes, one in New York, and one on Martha's Vineyard, a lovely island off Cape Cod, Massachusetts. When an announcement came through that a nuclear reactor was built in nearby Plymouth, Massachusetts, Carly and James publicly protested. In 1978 she gave a concert before an audience of 6,000 in Chillimark on Martha's Vineyard to raise funds to fight against the idea.

She's had a batch of big single hits. They include "That's The Way I've Always Heard It," "Legend In Your Own Time," and "You're So Vain." In 1977 she scored heavily again with a song from a James Bond movie, "Nobody Does It Better." For that song she was nominated "Best Female Performer" in the Grammy Awards. Her eight albums so far include: *Best of Carly Simon, Hotcakes, Playing Possum, Boys in the Trees* (on one track she has duet with hubby, James Taylor).

PAUL SIMON

Slim, 5'5", intense, with a sort of sad, serious look, Paul Simon continues to be a force in today's pop. He came up in the sixties as half of the team of Simon and Garfunkel. Now he's on his own, still turning out hits. Recently, he jumped from Columbia Records to Warner Records, partly because the new firm promised to let him act in and write films that would be produced by its film division. An added sweetener was a reported $15 million guaranteed royalty advance.

Though he's a performer who writes, Paul is not crazy about the trend. Once he told BMI's *World of Music*: "The emphasis that came in the sixties on the singer-songwriter—and I contributed to that—is one of the things wrong with music today. Nobody's just a songwriter or just a singer anymore. A good songwriter feels compelled to go out and be an artist and often he's so mediocre."

Following this logic, Simon perhaps is a better songwriter than singer-guitarist. However, it can also be argued that a songwriter singing his own songs adds a little something special. It's nice to hear the creator perform his own material, if he/she is talented.

Paul was born in Queens, N.Y., Oct. 13, 1941, where he met Art Garfunkel. They met first in a P.S. 164 musical production of *Alice in Wonderland.* Paul played Peter Rabbit and sang the Disney tune, "I'm Late, I'm Late for a Very Important Date." Later, the two took in rock shows at the Apollo Theatre and the New York Paramount. At 15 they came up with a teen hit, "Hey, Schoolgirl," as Tom and Jerry. After high school, Paul majored in English literature at Queens College, and Art studied math and education at Columbia. But they still continued to cut records and perform wherever they could in folk clubs (Gerde's, N.Y.) and in England. In 1964 they were signed by Columbia and taped an LP, *Wednesday Morning 3 A.M.*, a collection of folk songs plus Simon originals. A single from that LP was "Sounds of Silence." It was released (with added amplified beat) and became a number-one hit.

In those early songs, Simon showcased his musical personality, soft madrigal-type tunes, poetical lyrics, and a watchful eye on contemporary life. He's changed through the years, dipping into other music such as light jazz, pop, soft rock, gospel, reggae, but still there is a gentleness in his music, and a gift for catchy titles. His hits include: "Sounds of Silence," "Scarborough Fair Canticle," "Feelin' Groovy," "Mrs. Robinson," "50 Ways to Leave Your Lover," "Bridge Over Troubled Water" (a modern spiritual), and "Slip, Sliding Away."

Since he's been such a successful songwriter, it

might be wise to add this bit of advice on song-writing by Paul: "Simplicity is crucial," he says. "That's the sign of a good song. The less words you can say it in, the better off it really is."

Divorced, he's the father of a small boy. He thinks highly of the great show-music writers for Broadway. His first solo LP was released in 1972, and was titled *Paul Simon*. He still does teen-type stuff like "Me and Julio Down by the Schoolyard." He appeared briefly in Woody Allen's film, *Annie Hall* as a hip record-producer.

Paul on LP: *Greatest Hits*.

★

FRANK SINATRA

★

In October 1978 New York City TV newscasts showed a long line outside of Radio City Music Hall. Teenagers, young people in their twenties, middle-aged people, and gray-haired folk were standing in line, some huddled in blankets. They were spending the night on the sidewalk waiting for the box office to open so they could buy tickets to a week-long series of Frank Sinatra concerts. More than 6,000 tickets were sold in nine minutes. Ol' Blue Eyes still has that fantastic appeal.

No longer a thin-faced crooner of the late thirties, Sinatra is now almost plump, with graying hair. He is a grandpa, but not the kind that sits around the porch. He still is a force in pop—a magical singer with taste, savvy; a master at interpreting some of the best songs turned out by Tin Pan Alley, Broadway, and Hollywood. And to keep up, he even includes newer material by contemporary tunesmiths.

Rock dominates today's world of pop, but Sinatra continues to be an American show business phenomenon. He has been a star for more than 40 years, not only on records, but on TV, radio, in Hollywood, nightclubs, and concerts. In the total entertainment picture he is perhaps bigger than the Rolling Stones, the late Elvis Presley, and in a sense, the Beatles, though the Beatles scored extra points as songwriters too.

Even today's rockers and rock critics pay homage to him. In "The Scene" Lou Neil, Jr., the *New York Post*'s pop columnist, praised Sinatra's concert at Radio City Music Hall. Under the headline: MUSIC HALL TRIUMPH FOR OLD BLUE EYES he wrote: "At his triumphant return to Radio City Music Hall last week, Frank Sinatra put on one of the greatest concerts we have ever seen. In all the years we have covered the star, his voice never sounded finer. Loose as a goose, mellow, and very relaxed. Sinatra was at his best with numbers like 'Night and Day,' 'The Lady Is a Tramp,' 'Maybe This Time,' and 'Tender Trap.' His phrasing, inflection, poise, swing, and style have no comparison in entertainment."

The singer-actor-businessman-producer was born in Hoboken, N.J., Dec. 12, 1917. He started out with the idea of becoming a newspaperman, but switched to singing when he heard pop singers make more money. He was once a member of a pop group, the Hoboken Four, which won first prize on The Major Bowes Amateur Hour. His first real job was as a headwaiter and singer in a New Jersey night club for $15 a week.

He has acted in many films, musicals, dramas, and comedies. He won an Academy Award for a role in *From Here to Eternity*. Musical movies:

Higher and Higher, Anchors Aweigh, Till the Clouds Roll By, Take Me Out to the Ballgame, On the Town, High Society, Guys and Dolls, Can Can. Among his LPs, which are classics of the popular song art: *All the Way, Greatest Hits, Nice 'n' Easy, That's Life, September of My Years, Come Swing with Me.*

PATTI SMITH

"I went into rock and roll because it gives me carte blanche of where to put my music," says Patti Smith. "There's rock in dentists' offices, airplanes, and even bank robberies. I want our stuff to have everything in it. I want every grandmother, five-year-old, and Chinaman to be able to listen to it and say, 'Yeah.'"

Patti Smith *is* making some headway in rock. Basically, she is an experimental poet who's gone into rock. She believes that she can use rock to get her ideas across (and make money). Today, modern poetry reaches few people. Patti isn't content with this small audience; she wants to reach the masses. But so far, the masses haven't bought her. She's recorded several albums, and has had one hit single so far, "Because the Night."

However, she has a big media reputation far beyond her record sales. She's constantly written up in the pop music magazines such as *The Hit Parader*, and her concerts are reviewed with respect, if not admiration. She's an example of an artist who has a strong underground reputation, despite limited airplay.

Wild and drawn-looking, she could pose for a poster warning you of the dangers of not eating. She dresses funky, and her lyrics sometimes have "dirty words." She sings with a raw power, plays electric guitar, and heads an all-male band.

Some have called this native of New Jersey "the pin-up girl of punk rock." She is, however, a little too complicated to be put into any category. She blends a lot of influences: pop songs, cabaret, experimental writing.

Back in 1974 she gave a show at Reno Sweeney, a big hangout in Greenwich Village. The show was a typically odd mix. She came out dressed in a black satin pantsuit and elegant white satin blouse. She read some of her own poems, sang show songs ("Speak Low"), and gave a tribute to Ava Gardner, the actress. She also sang Cole Porter's "I Get a Kick Out of You," which she dedicated to Frank Sinatra, whom she described as the "Picasso of America."

In recent years, her concerts are more rock-oriented, but she still reads selections of her poetry ("Babel") and does pop shtick. At a recent concert in Chicago, she sang the Debby Boone hit, "You Light Up My Life," just to show that she can sing straight out too. She's hip to the world of record charts and disc jockeys. "Patti," wrote the *New York Post*, "is crazy, irritating, dishonest, brazen, frail, ambitious, bombastic, sweet, daring, and dedicated. That pile. . .has yet to be sorted out."

Her songs include: "Ain't It Strange," "Free Money,' "Ask the Angels," "So You Want to Be a Rock and Roll Star." Her LPs include: *Easter* (Arista) and *Horses*.

BRUCE SPRINGSTEEN

★

"Are you ready? . . . . Rock's come home." The words are from Bruce Springsteen as he does a local date at the Capitol Theatre in Passaic, New Jersey. A working-class street kid, Bruce's songs describe the frustrations of small-town life. Born Sept. 23, 1949, the 5'9" performer has brown eyes, dark brown hair, and weighs about 155. On stage he prowls like a cat, thumping his guitar and grimacing.

His father worked in a New Jersey factory; his mother, a housewife. They lived in Freehold. "Mom was an Elvis Presley fan. I remember," he once told WNEW's Dave Herman, "coming down for school when I was around nine and she'd be listening to the radio while she was cooking up the breakfast. Something connected then."

Not long after, Bruce started playing guitar. At 14, he had his own pickup band, but since then

he has only worked as a pop musician. He has had no other job. In the early seventies Bruce evolved as a guitarist and singer. He worked for little pay in the unglamorous bars and nightclubs in and around the Jersey coast. Today he is a Columbia recording star, and a big in-demand concert performer.

There's something wild about him. Most stars go on stage and do 75 minutes. Bruce has gone on stage and kept on going for 3½ hours. 3½ hours of high voltage rock. He must carry lots of insurance. One of his bits at concerts is making a flying leap into the audience.

His first LP, *Born to Run*, was produced by John Hammond (who discovered jazz singer Billie Holiday, and Bob Dylan) in 1973. With the release of his first LP, *Time* and *Newsweek* went wild over him. Then there was a long gap between records, mostly because of a law suit between Bruce and the people who had managed him. It took almost five years to untangle the legal hassle. In 1978 he came back strong with *Darkness on the Edge of Town*.

One of his LPs, *Born to Run*, took almost two years to finish. Some of his tunes have been recorded by other artists. Not long ago, Patti Smith had a Top-10 hit with a Springsteen composition, "Because of the Night." His backup musicians are bassist Gary Tallent, organist Danny Frederici, pianist Roy Bittan, drummer Max Weinberg, guitarist Steve Van Zandt, and sax man Clarence Clemmons. Bruce and Company are no longer East Coast names. They are now playing arenas and auditoriums all over.

He speaks softly. He is partial to tank tops and to the world of rock. It's his whole life. "I think I was lucky to find something that meant to much to me, as young as I was," he says. "I wish that luck on everybody."

His LPs include: *The Wild, The Innocent,* and *E-Street Shuffle.*

ROD STEWART

Thin with floppy, longish blond hair and a biggish nose, Rod Stewart is one of today's top singer-songwriters. He once told disc jockey Dave Herman over DIR Broadcasting: "I'm more in love with rock and roll than I am with any particular woman, or getting married. Other than play soccer, rock and roll is what I want to do."

Born Roderick David Stewart on Jan. 10, 1945, in Highgate, London, of Scottish parents, Rod played soccer as a teenager (he was once signed to a British pro team). Off the field he played harmonica. At 17 he left home and hitchhiked across Europe, spending much of his time in Italy and Spain.

Returning to England, he took his first music job at 19, playing harmonica with Jimmy Powell's Five Dimensions. That band played intermissions and supported the Rolling Stones in the very active British R & B scene of the 1960s. The white blues man, John Baldry, gave him his first chance as a vocalist.

"I had heard Rod before," Baldry remembers, "playing harmonica, but never singing. I discovered him at Twickenham railway station waiting for a train. Roddy was sitting on the platform, singing the blues. He rather impressed me so I asked him if he'd fancy a gig. So Rod joined my band as a vocalist."

A powerhouse singer of raw intensity, Rod worked with other groups after that, including Jeff Beck's and the Faces. Later on he turned solo recording artist on Mercury. He cracked through really big on his own in 1971 with a number-one single, "Maggie May," and an LP, *Every Picture Tells a Story.*

On stage, he swaggers and prances around like a wild man. He carries a fantastic light and audio system when on tour. He sings, one critic wrote, "with masculine authority." In May 1975, he signed with Warner Bros. and took up residence in Los Angeles. His debut album for that label, *Atlantic Crossing,* went gold quickly. Out of the LP came a global hit single, "Sailin'." In '76 he followed that up with a tremendous number-one single, "Tonight's the Night." As a songwriter he did himself proud with another hit, "The Killing of Georgie." In 1979 he was hotter than ever with a best-selling album, *Blondes Have More Fun* and a number-one single, "Do Ya Think I'm Sexy?"

His LPs (more than 16) include: *The Rod Stewart Album, Gasoline Alley, A Night on the Town, Foot Loose and Fancy Free, Long Player,* and *Ooh La La.*

BARBRA
STREISAND

"**E**ven when I was a kid," she once said, "I had to be somebody." Barbra was born in Brooklyn, N.Y., on April 24, 1942. From the time she could toddle she started performing, stealing her mother's lipstick to make up her face, then sitting before the TV set imitating commercials. She never had singing or ballet lessons, but she sang incessantly and toe-danced her way around the family apartment.

She graduated with honors from Erasmus Hall High School. While still in high school, Barbra attended several Manhattan acting schools. After a few weeks of summer stock she moved into a Manhattan apartment. She auditioned for many Broadway shows, even musicals, though she had never had a vocal lesson in her life. Barbra's first break occurred when she entered a talent contest in a Greenwich Village nightclub and won. A few

weeks later she was signed to sing at the Bon Soir, another Village night club.

When she moved to the Blue Angel, the word soon spread that the person to see and hear when you were in New York was a kooky young girl whose repertoire was composed mostly of unfamiliar songs. That led to an appearance on a talk show, *Mike Wallace PM East.*

Her Brooklynese accent, her thrift shop clothes and good humor brightened up the tube and gave her valuable exposure. It was while appearing at the Blue Angel that David Merrick, the Broadway producer of *I Can Get It for You Wholesale,* saw her.

She won a tiny part in that show, singing a song called "Miss Marmelstein," about the life of a secretary. When the LP of that show came out, *The New York Times* wrote, "The LP will go down in history as the advent of a great new singer."

Her voice can be warm, soft, and lyrical, as well as comic and raucous. She can belt too. Some of her records are marvels of pop singing ("People," "The Way We Were"). Her one weakness is a tendency to overdramatize a lyric. Her most successful musical role so far was in the Broadway version of *Funny Girl.* Once mostly a singer of Broadway theater-type songs, she now records mostly contemporary pop and rock, which bothers many show music fans.

Of course, Barbra is now a Hollywood star who does straight dramatic pictures *(The Way We Were),* screwball comedies *(What's Up Doc?),* as well as musical films like *Funny Girl* and *A Star Is Born.* Most musical comedy stars sell only in connection with an original cast album. Not Barbra. She's had an independently successful recording career with a string of Top-10 singles and best-selling LPs. Lately she's started to write. She is co-author of a Grammy Award winning song, "Evergreen," the love theme from *A Star Is Born*, an awful film. In Hollywood, she is known as a tough, iron-willed, "take charge" woman. Formerly married to Elliot Gould, she has a 14-year-old son, Jason. Her longtime boyfriend is an ex-hairdresser named Jon Peters.

Barbra on LP: *Funny Girl* (Broadway Original Cast Album), *Barbra's Greatest Hits* (Vol. 1, Vol. 2), *Songbird*, *A Star Is Born* (soundtrack), *Lazy Afternoon*, *Superman*, *The Way We Were*.

★

DONNA SUMMER

★

Many in the pop music business looked down on disco, thought it was a fad that would die out like a Fourth of July sparkler. But it's become a spectacular craze. There are now disco sections in record stores, all-disco radio stations, disco fashions, and glamorous disco clubs. Also separate disco divisions of record companies. Of course, it all got a big push by the disco dancing of John Travolta in *Saturday Night Fever.* But probably the big blaze was started by Donna Summer on a small label (now much bigger), Casablanca Records. She did it with a 17-minute record, "Love to Love Ya, Baby."

US magazine calls her the "queen of sex rock." Donna has also done personal appearances and TV. Not long ago, she was in a sort of disco comedy (produced by Casablanca Records), *Thank God It's Friday.*

Her singing style is locked firmly into disco by audience demand. In a review of her LP, *I Remember Yesterday, Variety* wrote that "unlike

many of the screaming disco singers, she is more than just a pretty good singer as she displays on her ballads. But what audiences want from Summer is something to dance to with a lot of beat, a lot of noise, and a lot of implied sex."

A black singer with a longish face and thin arms, Donna is a divorced mother of a five-year-old daughter. Her albums include: *Four Seasons of Love, I Remember Yesterday, Once Upon a Time.* Her singles include: "Last Dance" and "I Feel Love."

A few years ago, she was just knocking around, not getting anywhere until Bogart, president of Casablanca Records, decided to take a chance on her with a sort of marathon dance record, "Love to Love Ya, Baby." It was full of energy, little lyric. It caught on. The record sold like mad, and was featured at discotheques. Now she's trying to make her early success stand up and broaden her horizons a little. But that's hard since she's boxed in by her disco reputation. Besides new songs, she does disco versions of hits such as the Beatles' "I Remember Yesterday."

One of the few recording acts to make a successful transition to "live" in personal engagements, Donna gives quite a show. Though she sometimes does softer ballads on records, when she appears "live" she turns into a whirl of vocal energy, a disco dervish.

Not long ago, she did an in-person gig at the Felt Forum in New York. The *New York Post* wrote: "She is at best when belting and shouting at the crowd she has brought to its feet; she is not one for tender sweet ballads, or demonstrating control of range.

"Miss Summer got her disco audience to grunt and groan and sing along with her and eventually to dance at their seats. Its tacky and tasteless, all right. And someday we'll wonder what that music was all about."

Donna on LP: *I Remember Yesterday, Once Upon a Time, Live and More, Love to Love Ya, Baby, Love Trilogy.*

JAMES TAYLOR

He was a Beatles discovery. In 1968 he was the first artist signed to their firm, Apple Records, the first "outside act," and two of the Beatles accompanied him on his first recording. Taylor remembers, "It was an incredible time. I recorded my album while they were making the *White Album*. McCartney played bass on 'Carolina on My Mind' and George Harrison sang on another song. It was terrific, too good to be true."

But that LP, *James Taylor*, didn't sell. So Taylor eventually left Apple. Shortly after that, without the Beatles accompanying him, without the Beatles behind him, he cut an LP, *Sweet Baby James*, an LP that sold more than 3 million copies, which shows that show biz can be very strange. The Beatles opened doors for him but they couldn't make him an instant success.

James Taylor is presently one of the big contemporary singer-songwriters. He specializes in the soft sound, the poetic lyric. The star is very appealing to those who feel left out of the hard rock explosion. Sensitive, he looks like an intense poet with long hair and a slight mustache. He's married to Carly Simon. Summers they spend (when not touring) on Martha's Vineyard. Once on Apple, later on Warner Bros. Records, he now records for Columbia. In 1978 his debut album on his new label, *JT*, reached the Top-10.

As a boy, this earnest-looking singer-song-writer-guitarist would sing together with his three brothers and his sister, Kate. The young Taylors also played harmonica and listened to Woody Guthrie and Beethoven records, and to rhythm and blues and country music on the radio. That's some of the early musical roots of Taylor, son of a medical executive, born Mar. 20, 1948. He grew up in the Bible Belt, in a contemporary ranch house outside of Chapel Hill, North Carolina. His father was dean of the medical school at the University of North Carolina. He graduated from high school, toyed with the idea of continuing on to college but instead jobbed around as a performer in Greenwich Village. A friend of his got word to Peter Asher of Apple Records, the Beatle firm, about Taylor's singing and songs.

A complicated personality, he has had drug problems and has been in and out of psychiatric institutions. His lyrics are introspective, moody, and they are set in a contemporary folk/rock style. *The New York Times* once said of him, "He sings quietly, which is unique in our times." A rock writer has observed, "He's not five frenzied speed freaks blowing your eardrums with amplifiers because they can't blow your minds with a strong emotional message." His songs include "Fire and

Rain," "Hey, Mister, That's Me Up on the Jukebox," and "Sunny Skies."

Not exactly an activist, he has come out strongly against nuclear power. "I am usually cautious about lending my name to causes in general, but in the case of nuclear power, I feel that the health of the planet is at stake," he has said. "I speak also for my wife, Carly. We are parents of two young children [Sarah, Benjamin] and it is our concern that they be able to grow up in a world which is not poisonous."

On LP: *Mud Slide Slim, One Man Dog, Walking Man, In the Pocket*. Film: *Two Lane Blacktop*.

JOHN TRAVOLTA

Ever since the birth of sound in 1929, Hollywood has come up with hit songs, best-selling soundtracks, and musical comedy stars. We've all enjoyed Fred Astaire, Gene Kelly, Judy Garland, Bing Crosby. The latest star to come out of films is John Travolta.

He doesn't have a terrific way with a song, but he can act and he can dance. He's been connected with two of the best-selling soundtracks of all time, *Saturday Night Fever* and *Grease.*

In *Grease* he sang "Sandy." In that film he also sang a duet with Olivia Newton-John, "You're the One That I Want." It turned into a platinum single and was number one on many record charts.

Six-foot Travolta, of course, was first spotted as Vinnie Barbarino in *Welcome Back, Kotter,* a TV sitcom. His birthdate is Feb. 18. He weighs about 178 pounds. His hair is brown and his eyes are blue.

John Travolta is one of six children of Helen and

Salvatore Travolta. He started his acting career at his mother's encouragement—she had been active as a drama teacher, director, and actress for more than 20 years. Born in Englewood, New Jersey, John attended Dwight Morrow High School until he turned 16. He quit school in order to pursue a more active career in the theater. His first stage role was in *Who Will Save the Plowboy?* at the New Dimension Theatre.

Fresh from his first role after taking voice and dancing lessons, John found himself in an off-Broadway production of *Rain*. From there it was straight to Broadway and his appearance in *Grease*. After touring with the company for ten months, he returned to Broadway in the Andrews Sisters show, *Over Here*, for another ten months.

His television credits include *Emergency; Owen Marshall, Counsellor at Law; The Rookies;* and *Medical Center*. He also had the starring role in the highly acclaimed *The Boy in the Plastic Bubble*, a special movie presentation which aired on ABC. John has also won roles in *Carrie* and *Moment By Moment*. In his latest film, *Urban Cowboy*, he does several musical numbers.

Travolta lives in Santa Barbara, California. He spends much of his free time flying his own two-seat single-engine Ercoupe.

The sensitive-looking actor-singer-dancer has been attacked by East Germany as an "insidious influence on youth." Wrote a German newspaper: "Travolta tries to make capitalist daily life seem harmless." "The anti-Travolta barbs," added *The New York Times*, "were obviously aimed at dampening Travolta's rising popularity in East Germany where discotheques feature music from his movies, and magazines from the West with the actor's picture on them are a hot item."

John on LP (solo): *John Travolta* and *Can't Let You Go.*

THE
VILLAGE PEOPLE

★

Casablanca Records is named after the famous
Humphrey Bogart movie. That's because the
head of it is Neil Bogart. He runs quite a mini-
conglomerate: records, films, Broadway musicals.
He's had a hand in co-producing *FM* (movie and
best-selling soundtrack), the cast album of the
Broadway hit, *They're Playing Our Song*, and
many other hit recordings, including those of Kiss.
But perhaps Bogart's biggest splash has been in the
disco field with Donna Summer and such groups
as The Village People.

The Village People are an energetic vocal/dance
disco group. Naturally they wear crazy costumes
in live appearances: boots, shiny jump suits, Indian headdresses, hard hats and flannel checked
shirts, cowboy hats and jeans. The young combo
immediately caught on with their first records. In
'78 the trade papers (*Billboard, Record World,*

Cash Box) who put out yearly evaluations have included them or their recordings in such categories as "Disco Artist of the Year," "Disco Album of the Year," "Disco Cross-Over Artists of the Year." The categories are confusing. But they indicate that the group has caught on at the record counters.

Teen Heroes described "Macho Man" as a "joyful celebration of a liberated life-style" (whatever that is). Their other hits include "YMCA" (which the YMCA objected to) and "In the Navy."

Who are The Village People? They are six singer-dancers. One of them, Victor Willis, comes from Broadway musical comedy. He's appeared in several shows including *The Wiz*. Randy Jones has acted on TV and danced with many dance companies before he hooked up with The Village People. Glen Hughes has done some acting. Another member, David "Scar" Hodo, used to do shtick to break into show business. Once he appeared on *What's My Line* on roller skates while "eating" fire. Felipe Rose's background is the dance. Rounding out the hit group is Alexander Briley, a singer.

You can see The Village People in the movies. Allan Carr, co-producer of *Grease*, produced a musical with them, *Can't Stop the Music*. In the film are new songs as well as the group's top hits, which of course are recycled into a soundtrack album.

THE WHO

Recently *Record World* ran this headline: "1979: *Year of the Who*." If you recall, the British group was badly shaken by the death of drummer Keith Moon, in September 1978, from an overdose of drugs. For a while the group seemed to be in a daze. But now the remaining members, Peter Townsend (lead guitarist born May 9, 1945), Roger Daltrey (lead singer born Mar. 1, 1944), and John Entwhistle (bass guitarist, born Oct. 9, 1944) have been functioning with subs on percussion. Not long ago, they released an LP on MCA, formerly Decca Records, *Who Are You?*

In '79 there was a flurry of activity with the release of two films and two accompanying sound-track albums with strong commercial potential. One film is *Quadrophenia*, for which the original members of the Who (Peter, John, and Roger) acted as producers but do not appear in the film. The second feature has a catchy title, *The Kids Are Alright*. It's a documentary about the group with coverage of "live" concerts and studio sessions. The soundtrack album is reported to include portions of their famed rock opera, *Tommy*, as well as *A Quick One*, a capsule work of musical theater, plus pop songs, including "Happy Jack" and "Anyway, Anyhow, Anywhere."

In April '79, lean, long-faced Pete Townsend said, "At the moment we're trying to put together what looks to be the craziest, busiest, most lunatic year of our whole career."

At the same time, Peter is planning to go solo. He's signed with Atco. "When I say solo, I mean it will be solo album. A good drummer, that's all I need." Whether the Who will tour to back up its album releases remains up in the air. "I'm not interested in intense exposure. I'm not hungry enough to sacrifice everything anymore," he says.

Members of the Who grew up in roughly the same part of London—Shepherd's Bush. There's no bush there; it's citified, urban. School played a big role in the birth of the British group. Roger and John met in the English equivalent of a U.S. high school and formed the Detours, a real nonsuccess. Later, Pete joined the group, and they practiced a good deal in Pete's garage. Somehow they decided to change their name to the High Numbers, and at this stage Keith Moon joined them, and after a while they changed their name for another attention-getter, the Who. At first the group begged audiences to watch them at a place called the Marquee Club. Signs said, "Please come in, no strings attached." In 1964 they started winning audience acclaim with their version of rock.

They finally made the British pop scene with their first hit in 1964, "I Can't Explain."

The Who on LP: *My Generation, Happy Jack, The Who Sell Out, Magic Bus, Tommy, Live at Leeds.*

TAMMY
WYNETTE

★

In 1964 she was living in a rundown, 60-year-old, three-room house on a Mississippi farm. It had no indoor plumbing, no way to pump water, and no stove. She cooked in an open fireplace, carried her water from a spring down the hill, and boiled diapers in an iron pot over a backyard fire.

Now Tammy is a star singer-songwriter. Her music and her steely determination to succeed has helped her rise from poverty. There are broken hearts all along Nashville's Tin Pan Alley, but not hers. Her home is a 9½-acre estate in Nashville with 14 bathrooms, a swimming pool, and tennis court. She also has a 10-room French Regency beach house in Jupiter, Florida.

On the average she spends about 15 days a month on the road. She crisscrosses the country in a $200,000 bus doing fairs and one-nighters. *Chicago Tribune* columnist, Jack Hurt, calls her "one of the greatest vocal stylists of our time." In a book, *Singers and Sweethearts,* Tammy is praised for her "tearful singing style."

A naive farm girl who had never been inside a recording studio, she cut her first single ("Apt. #9") in 1966. Tammy has gone on to sell more than 18 million records, grossing more than $60 million. Her recording of "Stand By Your Man" is the biggest-selling single in the history of country music. She's been number-one on the charts 35 times. The first female country artist to receive a platinum album for sales exceeding one million albums (as certified by the R.I.A.A.), Tammy has won two Grammys and is a three-time winner of the Country Music Association's Top Female Vocalist of the Year Award. In 1976 Great Britain named her Number-One Female Vocalist of England.

She was born Virginia Wynette Pugh on May 5, 1942, on her grandfather's cotton farm in Mississippi. By age seven, Tammy was working the cotton fields along with other relatives on the farm. "Hoeing, chopping, picking, and hating every minute of it," she recalls. She was a teenage bride, and had two children quickly. Her husband was a construction worker, often unemployed. At one time she lived in a shack with huge cracks in the walls. Tammy says she "insulated them with cardboard boxes I ripped up and nailed to the walls."

Tammy later became a beautician, and then turned to singing. She moved to Nashville and there she got a break with Epic Records. Now divorced, she's been married four times (once to country singer George Jones) and has four children.

Tammy has developed into quite a songwriter. She writes both on guitar and piano. Tammy considers writing "a form of therapy .... the best way I know to get something off my chest."

Tammy on LP: *Greatest Hits* (Vol. 1, 2, 3, 4), *One of a Kind, Womanhood.*

NEIL YOUNG

From Canada (born Nov. 12, 1945), this singer-guitarist-songwriter grew up in Toronto and Winnipeg. His father was a sportswriter on the *Toronto Telegram*. When Neil was 14 he bought Neil a ukulele, a tinkly instrument with a joyful sound, popularized by Arthur Godfrey, then a star on U.S. radio. That started Neil off. It's believed that the first song he learned was "God Save the Queen."

In his high school years, he played at local affairs around Winnipeg for $50 or so with a group called the Squires. With fellow musicians, he made his way to Toronto in an old Buick hearse, which broke down just as it reached the city. In Yorkville, a sort of Greenwich Village type of neighborhood in Toronto, he formed a group called the Mynah Birds. But jobs were few and Neil had to take a job in a bookstore.

Borrowing $400 from his father, he decided to try to break into the California music scene. In Los Angeles, he met some musicians in a hamburger place. this led to the formation of the Buffalo Springfield. In 1967 the group—known for its close-knit inventive harmonies—took off. It recorded a series of successful soft-rock LPs including *Buffalo Springfield, Buffalo Springfield Again,* and *Last Time Around.* For the new group, Neil wrote a hit song,, "For All It's Worth."

Eventually, the band broke up. Later Neil was asked to join another group which recorded under the name of Crosby, Stills, Nash, and Young (*Déjà Vu, Four-Way Street, The All-American Record Album*). That was a loose group that permitted its members to do things on their own too. In 1969 Neil made the first of a series of solo albums, starting with *Neil Young* on Warner Reprise.

His roots are folk music, but he also does powerful hard rock. His songs focus on a variety of topics, love ("Tonight's the Night"), as well as social-political material ("Cortez, the Killer"), and intriguing comment ("Darling, It's the Media").

Among his most popular works was a bestselling gold record, *After the Gold Rush.* In a review, one critic wrote: "Words like lovely, beautiful and romantic, cannot often be applied to rock albums except such LPs as Neil Young's *After the Gold Rush.* It is a delicate fragile jewel." In one of his later albums, *Comes a Time*, he returned to folk music.

He likes the outdoor life, building things with his hands. He lives in California on a cattle ranch. In March '79 plans were announced for Neil to tour with a group called the Barbarians. Among those scheduled to participate were Keith Richards and Ron Wood of the Rolling Stones.

His single hits include: "Heart of Gold," "Old Man," and "War Song." His solo albums include: *Everybody Knows This Is Nowhere*, *Harvest*, *Journey Through the Past* (film soundtrack), *On the Beach*, *Zuma*, *American Stars 'n' Bars*, *Decade*, *Comes a Time*.